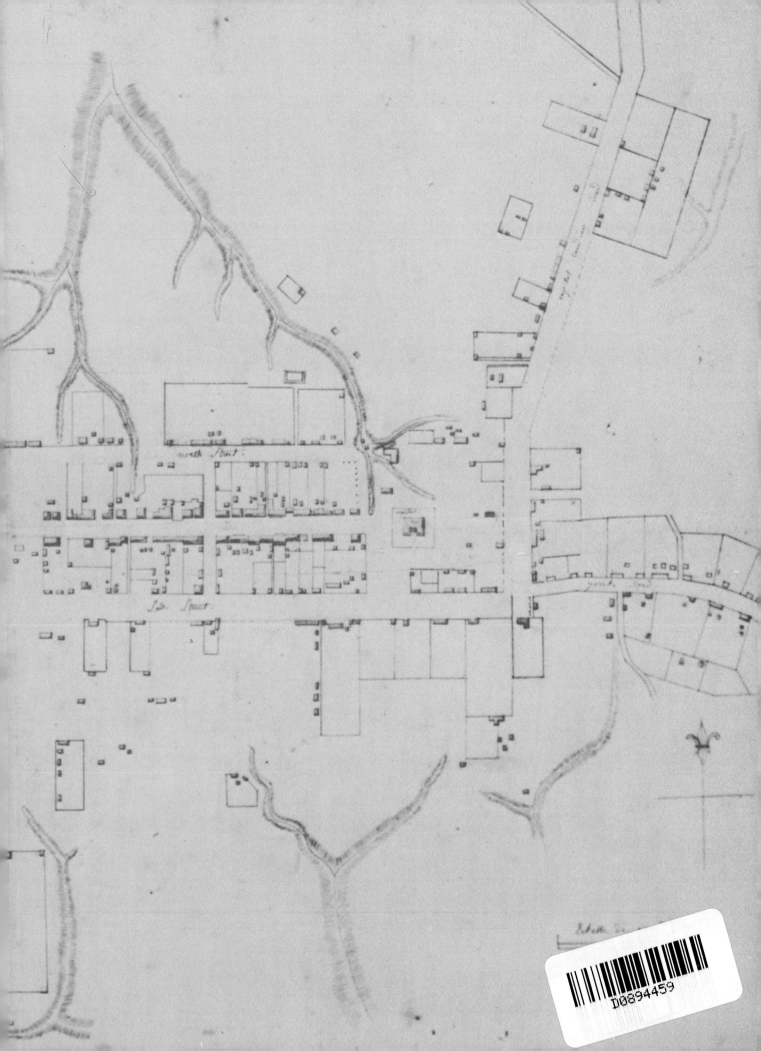

Hark Upon The Gale

The Spotswood Cannon, on the colonial campus, points toward College Corner. The Brafferton is in the background. Courtesy of the Office of University Communications, College of William and Mary

Hark Upon The Gale

The Donning Company/Publishers
Norfolk/Virginia Beach

An Illustrated History of
The College of William and Mary

By Wilford Kale

Foreword by Mills E. Godwin, Jr.

Copy photography by Nic Siler

In 1899 the first William and Mary yearbook included not only photographs of the classes, fraternities, and athletic groups, but also various clubs, including the bicycle club. The members included J. T. Garrow, R. O. Rogers, R. E. Henderson, R. M. Hughes, J. N. Hornbaker, G. Wyatt, E. B. Dennie, E. S. Phillips, E. J. Taylor, F. M. Mallory, D. B. Herbditch, N. Savedge, B. F. Epps, E. E. Stacey, R. W. Corbitt, J. H. Bonneville, J. C. Donovan, and H. H. Foster. The faculty sponsor was Professor H. S. Bird (right rear with moustache). From the 1899 Colonial Echo, *courtesy of the College Archives; College of William and Mary*

*For my special ladies—my wife, Louise;
my daughter, Anne-Evan;
and my mother, Martha.*

Every effort has been made to identify the owners of the
illustrations appearing in this book. Should there be any
omissions in this respect, we apologize and shall be pleased to
make the appropriate acknowledgments in any future printings.

The Donning Company/Publishers
5659 Virginia Beach Boulevard
Norfolk, Virginia 23502

Library of Congress Cataloging in Publication Data

Kale, Wilford, 1944-
    Hark upon the gale.

    Bibliography: p.
    Includes index.
    1. College of William and Mary—History.   I. Title.
II. Illustrated History of the College of William and Mary.
LD6051.W52K35   1984   378.755'4252   84-18848
ISBN 0-89865-397-5

Printed in the United States of America

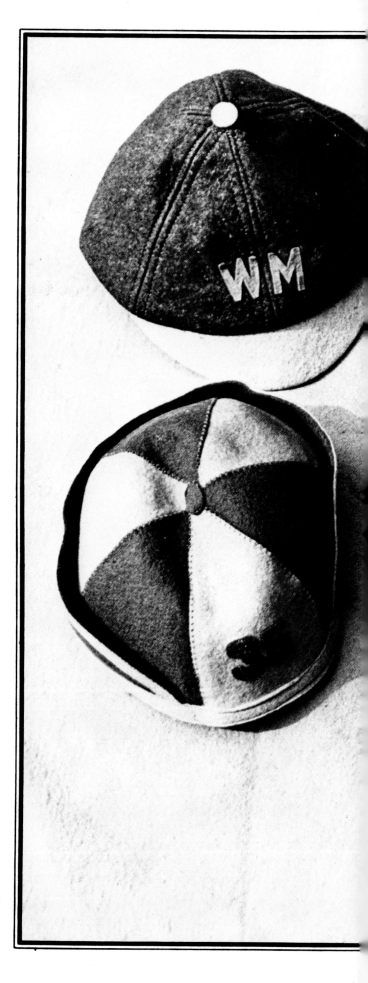

The term "duc," applied for many years to freshmen at the college, apparently goes back to the 1890s. From about 1888 until 1910 the college maintained subcollegiate work for those of its students who had not graduated from secondary schools. This subcollegiate work was generally listed in the catalogues as introductory work; the lowest class in English was introductory English, et cetera. It was quite natural for students to nominate first-year students taking these introductory courses as ducs, and the term stuck through the mid-1960s when Duc Week was phased out. This picture shows duc caps from various years. Courtesy of the Society of the Alumni

In 1893 the entire student body posed for a group photograph. Courtesy of the College Archives, College of William and Mary

Contents

This is an unretouched copy of the daguerreotype of the east face of the Sir Christopher Wren Building, taken about 1858 after substantial repairs had been made. It is the oldest known photograph of the college building and shows the second version of the building, constructed between 1709 and 1716. Note the large columns supporting the second floor balcony. The small trees were replacements newly planted for those large stately trees killed in the Dutch Elm blight of 1843. Courtesy of the College Archives, College of William and Mary

Foreword

For many years a reporter and Williamsburg bureau chief of the *Richmond Times-Dispatch*, Wilford Kale has been an astute observer of events at the College of William and Mary. This volume offers a penetrating look at the college's past and present from the perspective of one intimately familiar with its history. The author is a capable and respected reporter and writer. He is a native of North Carolina, but a longtime Virginian by choice; an honor graduate of Park College in Kansas City, Missouri; and an alumnus of the College of William and Mary.

From the vantage point of a student, news reporter, and one fascinated with its history, he has written many articles covering current happenings at the college and has contributed frequently to the pages of the *Alumni Gazette*. For nearly twenty years he has researched, studied, and assembled the information used in this book.

Those of us who are alumni and friends of the college are pleased that this concise and first illustrated history of the institution now becomes available not only to us but also to the general public. The illustrations range from eighteenth-century portraits and engravings to the first photograph of the college in 1858 and late nineteenth and early twentieth-century photographs. Many of them have never been previously published.

We are indebted to Wilford Kale for the story of this ancient college so aptly called the "Alma Mater of a Nation." William and Mary mightily influenced many of our early patriots who put together in Williamsburg the building blocks and foundation documents that were so vital to the birth of our nation.

The Commonwealth of Virginia is a crown of many jewels and none is more precious than the College of William and Mary. The author recalls for us here nearly three hundred years of its service to Virginia and to the nation. Indeed, this is a book full of intriguing history that you will wish to read, enjoy, and treasure.

—MILLS E. GODWIN, JR
Class of 1936
*Governor of Virginia
1966-1970, 1974-1978*

9

Preface

"Hark, the students' voices swelling,
Strong and true and clear,
Alma Mater's love they're telling
Ringing far and near.

"William and Mary, loved of old,
Hark upon the gale
Hear the thunder of our chorus,
Alma Mater—Hail!"

Those words of the William and Mary alma mater were penned by James Southall Wilson, class of 1902. Set to a familar tune they evoke the mystique that flavors the campus and many of the historical events that have taken place in its colorful past.

In this book, I have not endeavored to present a detailed, encompassing history, but rather to present a condensed view of the history of William and Mary combined in a pictorial form. This work could best be described as a "popular," rather than a "scholarly," account. There are many events and subjects which have been omitted, and I leave to historians the task of developing a detailed, encompassing, multivolume history of William and Mary. It is unfortunate that such a work has never been written.

I should thank Dr. Christian H. Moe, class of 1951, who wrote a play designed as William and Mary's contribution to the 350th anniversary of the Jamestown settlement. His 1957 drama about the college's history was entitled *Hark Upon the Gale,* and I have borrowed Dr. Moe's title for my book; I find no problem there, since he also borrowed it from a line in the alma mater.

This project was a labor of love! It involved examining hundreds of papers, pamphlets, booklets, theses, books, letters, minutes, and records related to the college. I became interested in the history of William and Mary almost from the first day I set foot on campus in September 1962. From random glances through the library stacks, to more careful and systematic quests in the college's archives, the history of William and Mary has unfolded for me.

There is, of course, going to be a certain bias associated with this work. I will give attention, maybe more than some feel is justified, to aspects of the history that I have found intriguing and will probably exclude some facets others believe have more meaning. Such is the nature of any look at the past.

I would like to thank many persons who encouraged me to develop this book through the five or so years of dreaming and preparing: the late Herbert Ganter, longtime William and Mary archivist, chronicler, and walking college encyclopedia; the late Dortha Skelton, longtime William and Mary reference librarian, who aided me, first as a student, later as a newspaper reporter, and finally as a writer; my late grandfather, "W.W." Kale, who constantly urged and prompted me to write a history; my late father, Wilford Kale, for his admonition to learn as much about the college as I possibly could; my father-in-law, J. Wilfred Lambert, longtime William and Mary dean of students; and my mother-in-law, Anne Nenzel Lambert.

I also would like to thank two Southern author friends, LeGette Blythe of Huntersville, North Carolina and Burke Davis, formerly of Williamsburg, for encouraging me to put my words not only in newsprint, but also in book form.

I would like to thank personnel at the Earl Gregg Swem Library, particularly Clifford Currie, librarian; Margaret Cook, curator of manuscripts and rare books; Kay Domine, archivist; and Laura Frances Parrish, assistant archivist. I also wish to thank the Colonial Williamsburg Foundation, including former senior vice president Donald J. Gonzales; Norman G. Beatty, vice president; and the foundation's audiovisual staff. Special appreciation goes to the late Thomas B. Schlesinger, who would not let me forget the idea.

Thanks to the members of the staff of the

Society of the Alumni, especially to Gordon C. Vliet, former society executive vice president; Susan Dunham, friend, yearbook provider and keen proofreader; Patricia Foran, business manager; Frankie Martens; and H. Westcott Cunningham, current executive vice president.

My appreciation for their invaluable assistance goes to former presidents of William and Mary: the late Dr. John Pomfret, Admiral Alvin Duke Chandler, and Dr. Davis Y. Paschall. Thanks also to college staff members S. Dean Olson, Charles Holloway, and Joe Gilley. Special thanks to Ross L. Weeks, Jr., William A. Molineux, and Wayne Barrett for listening and helping and to Susan Q. Bruno and Linda Collins Reilly who read the manuscript.

The Richmond Newspapers Inc., especially executive editor Alf Goodykoontz, was extremely helpful in providing resources and time to put this project together. Thanks also to *Richmond Times-Dispatch* managing editor Marvin Garrette and state editor Michael Steele.

Very special appreciation goes to Mary R. M. Goodwin for allowing me the use of several of her major research reports on the college, for reading the manuscript for historical accuracy, and for providing helpful suggestions.

Thanks to my editor Nancy Morgan who survived my journalistic writing style.

William and Mary has for 292 years survived the destruction of wars and fires, the ravages of failed finances and failed loyalties, and the insensitivities of careless people. This concise glimpse of William and Mary's history, like the 1957 drama, expresses the spirit of the school. In the drama's final scene, the character representing Dr. Lyon G. Tyler said:

"So let our college stand forever as a lasting symbol of patriotic service, of unshaken faith, of magnificent history which binds the glories of the past with the hopes of the future. . . . Hark upon the gale of history, my friends and listen to its call!"

This photograph is of the impression of the original, colonial seal of the College of William and Mary in Virginia; it is on a document issued by the college in 1749. It is the clearest and strongest impression available. Courtesy of the Manuscript and Rare Book Department, Swem Library, College of William and Mary; Henry Grunder photo

William of Orange married Mary,
daughter of King James II of England,
in 1677. They became William III and
Mary II of England in 1689 following
the "Glorious Revolution" which
ousted Mary's father, who was a
Catholic. William died in 1702 after a
hunting accident and was succeeded
by Mary's younger sister Anne.

This seventeenth century portrait
of King William III by Sir Godfrey
Kneller currently hangs in the front
hall of the President's House. Courtesy of the College Art Collection,
College of William and Mary;
Thomas L. Williams photo

Introduction

By Dr. Harold Lees Fowler

The marriage of William and Mary in 1677 was a purely political alliance, designed to bind the House of Orange and the House of Stuart closer together and to join England with the Dutch Republic in the defense of their mutual interests against the menace of France.

The marriage was never a happy one, even though Mary became devoted to her husband and obeyed his every wish. The fact is that husband and wife had little in common. Mary—taller and rather pretty, compliant, sociable, and talkative—was even younger than her years and wholly innocent in the affairs of the world. But in spite of William's humiliating, often insolent behavior, Mary was always the uncomplaining, self-sacrificing wife. It is true that shortly before her death she wrote a letter to her husband admonishing him for his infidelities and urging him to mend his ways. Beyond this final rebuke, one may surmise that Mary found some comfort from the fact that compared to her father, James II, and her uncle, Charles II, her husband was almost a saint.

Cut off from her home and friends, frequently separated from her husband for long intervals while he was engrossed in problems of state, Mary was a lonely young bride, spending her time playing cards (a diversion to which she became addicted), reading as much as her weak eyes would permit, and eating so much that she developed into a plump and heavy woman. Naturally amiable, and longing for companionship, she went out of her way to win the affection of the Dutch people; her sweet disposition, her strong sense of duty, and her genuine piety made her popular.

William, by contrast, was a cold, hard, forbidding man. He had none of the social graces; he never attempted to be affable even when it was to his political advantage. He was most uncommunicative and remained in seclusion as much as possible. John Evelyn speaks of his "morose temper" and his "coldness of manner." In fact, his manners seem to have given almost universal offense. He consciously avoided social intercourse and except for his fondness for hunting, he scorned ordinary amusements and diversions.

When it was necessary for him to appear at public functions or social gatherings he would stand off to one side surveying the assembly with a cold stare. Those who dared to engage him in conversation were rebuffed by curt remarks or biting sarcasm, and the unfortunate victims escaped as quickly as possible.

This forbidding portrait is almost totally unrelieved. There are scraps of evidence to indicate that at times he could be convivial in an intimate group of Dutch friends. His correspondence with his devoted friend Wiliam Bentinck shows that he was capable of flashes of warmth and kindness. But certainly the great majority of his contemporaries were unaware of this. Even when we turn to his relations with his wife, there is little evidence of real love or tenderness. There is some reason to believe that, until he became a king, William was jealous of his wife, for she was heir presumptive to a crown while he was merely a prince. At any rate, it was not a happy marriage despite Mary's deep devotion to her husband.

Whatever the truth may be regarding his feelings toward his wife, to almost everyone else in England he remained a most unpleasant and unpopular figure. He never loved England and he never obtained her love. He distrusted most of the politicians of the day, and with some good reason, for seldom has there been a time in English history when the level of political morality was so low. On the other hand, he could be most unfair; he made no distinction between those who served him well and those who served him ill.

In fairness to William it should be noted that constant poor health may have contributed to the unfortunate impression he made upon others. Born with a frail physique and a slight deformity of the back, he suffered throughout his life from asthma, and, toward the end, from tuberculosis. He had a terrible cough and could sleep only when propped up with pillows. The smog of London made life almost unbearable, and while he disliked court life anyway, this is perhaps the main reason why he and Mary decided to withdraw from Whitehall. Therefore, they moved to Hampton Court Palace, that magnificent structure a few miles away.

A companion portrait of Queen Mary II, also painted in the seventeenth century by Sir Godfrey Kneller, currently hangs in the front hall of the President's House. Mary Stuart was the daughter of James II and with her husband, William of Orange, succeeded to the English throne in 1689 following her father's exile. Mary II died of smallpox in 1694 at the age of 32. Courtesy of the College Art Collection, College of William and Mary; Thomas L. Williams photo

Under the direction of Sir Christopher Wren, major alterations and additions were undertaken. Mary took a personal interest in the renovation and enlargement of the building and in the planning of the gardens. Wren remarked upon her "exquisite judgment." Long before the work on Hampton Court was completed, William decided to purchase Nottingham House, a less pretentious edifice and more convenient to Whitehall. This was converted into Kensington Palace, which served as the residence of the royal couple until Mary's death.

Shocked at the plight of the English seamen disabled in the war with France, Mary suggested that the palace at Greenwich, started by her uncle, Charles II, but later discontinued, should now be completed to serve as a retreat for seamen injured in the service of their country. Her dream was not realized during her lifetime, but a few years later the majestic Greenwich Hospital, also designed by Wren, was completed and stands today as a memorial to Queen Mary.

It was partly her religious interest, plus her support of worthy charitable causes, that induced Mary to encourage the project for the founding of a college in Virginia. The Reverend James Blair reported to Governor Francis Nicholson, in December 1691, that when he first arrived in London to seek royal support to build a college, he naturally went to his superior, the Bishop of London, Henry Compton. But this was just at the moment when the bishop was so resentful at having been denied promotion to Canterbury that he was unwilling to go to court or make any approach to the king in favor of Blair's project.

Forced to change his tactics, Blair turned to the bishop of Worcester, who approached the queen on the subject of the college. Mary was not merely interested; she was enthusiastic and promised to recommend the proposal to the king, though she insisted that the presentation of the petition to the council be delayed until William could be present.

Arrangements were made for Blair to appear in the council chamber, November 12, 1691. He presented his petition for the founding of the college, and William gave his official approval in these words: "Sir, I am glad that the Colony is upon so good a design, and I will promote it to the best of my power."

The establishment of the college was now assured, but Blair's mission was not completed until February 8, 1693, when the charter creating the College of William and Mary in Virginia was granted. It may be concluded from Blair's testimony and that of Bishop (Gilbert) Burnet that Mary was primarily responsible for persuading William to endorse the founding of the college.

The queen was taken ill shortly before Christmas, 1694. At first it was thought to be an attack of measles, but by Christmas night her physicians knew it was the dread smallpox. William, fearing the worst from the outset, ordered a bed placed in her room so that he might remain by her side. She grew steadily weaker during the next forty-eight hours and died at 1:00 a.m., December 28, at the age of thirty-two. William remained a widower and died in May 1702.

In retrospect, no objective observer can accept Bishop Burnet's pronouncement that Mary "was the Glory of her Sex, the darling of human nature and the wonder of all that knew her." On the other hand, we may respect and admire her solid virtues: her charity, her deep religious faith, her devotion to her husband, and her self-sacrifice. Above all we may feel genuine sympathy for one whose short life was so darkened by sadness and suffering. Deprived of her mother at the age of nine, torn from home, family, and native land by a child-marriage to a man who learned to love her only when it was too late, impelled by circumstances largely beyond her control to break with her father, and, eventually, with her sister and uncle, her crowning sorrow was the denial of the blessings of motherhood, the supreme tragedy for a queen.

(The late Dr. Fowler was a member of the faculty of the History Department of the College of William and Mary from 1934 to 1974. He was Dean of the Faculty of Arts and Sciences from 1964 to 1974. His original address was delivered on February 8, 1968, the 275th anniversary of the granting of the royal charter. Permission to use a condensed version as the introduction to this book was given by his widow, Helen Abbott Fowler.)

Chapter One
1617-1693

A Foundation of Sorts

ILLIAM AND MARY, by the Grace of God, of *England, Scotland, France* and *Ireland,* King and Queen, Defenders of the Faith, &c. To all to whom these Our present Letters shall come, greeting:

"Forasmuch as our well-beloved and trusty Subjects, constituting the General Assembly of our Colony of *Virginia,* have had it in their Minds, and have proposed to themselves, to the end that the Church of *Virginia* may be furnish'd with a Seminary of Ministers of the Gospel, and that the Youth may be piously educated in good Letters and Manners, and that the Christian Faith may be propagated amongst the Western *Indians,* to the Glory of Almighty God, to make, found, and establish a certain Place of universal Study, or perpetual College of Divinity, Philosophy, Languages, and other good Arts and Sciences, consisting of one President, six Masters or Professors, and an hundred Scholars, more or less, according to the Ability of the said College . . .

". . . And further, we will, and for us, our Heirs and Successors, by these Presents do

The Reverend James Blair, a Scot who became an Anglican, was sent to Virginia on assignment from the bishop of London. Blair helped establish the College of William and Mary, and from its founding in 1693 until his death in 1743 served as the college's first president. This eighteenth century portrait and the one of his wife were painted in London during their 1703-1705 visit. Courtesy of the College Art Collection, College of William and Mary

grant, That when the said College shall be so erected, made, founded, and established, it shall be called and denominated for ever, *The College of* William *and* Mary *in Virginia;* . . . ."

With those words from the royal charter granted by King William III and Queen Mary II of England, the College of William and Mary in Virginia was established February 8, 1693, with the Reverend James Blair, commissary of the bishop of London in Virginia, as its first president.

The establishment of a college in Virginia was an important event for the colony, but William and Mary was not the first such attempt. As early as 1617, efforts had been made by the clergy in England to raise funds to found a college to educate and train the Indians and to lay "the foundation of a seminary of learning for the English." In 1619, King James I encouraged the activity and about 1,500 pounds was collected and turned over to the Virginia Company of London, which would help erect the school.

In fact, the Virginia Company, a year earlier, at the urging of Sir Edwin Sandys, treasurer of the company, had ordered that 10,000 acres within the Corporation of Henrico be set aside for the support of the college, and about 100 men sent from England to be tenants. Rents from the property, worth about 500 pounds a year, would allow for the buildings to be erected and the teachers paid. George Thorpe, a gentleman of the king's privy chamber, was engaged to travel to Virginia to become superintendent of the college.

Meanwhile, in Virginia, people became interested in the establishment of a public free

Sarah Harrison Blair, who married the Reverend James Blair in 1687, was the daughter of Benjamin Harrison of Wakefield. Courtesy of the College Art Collection, College of William and Mary

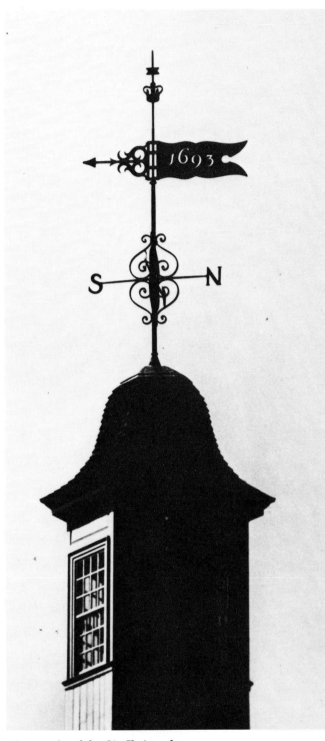

The cupola of the Sir Christopher Wren Building, the principal building of William and Mary, contains the school bell, which now tolls on the hour. For much of the school's history the bell also rang for changes of class. A modern-day weathervane notes the date—1693—of the founding of the college. Thomas L. Williams photo

school. With plans rapidly proceeding for a college, it was decided by the Virginia Company that the "East India School" be established at Charles City and that such a free school "should have dependence upon the Colledge in Virginia which should be made capable to receive Scholars from the Schoole into such Scollerships and fellowshipps as the said Colledge shall be endowed with all for the advancement of Schollers as they arise by degrees and deserts in learning."

As John Jennings detailed in his volume, *The Library of the College of William and Mary in Virginia, 1693-1793*, the university at Henrico "was planned not only as a missionary college for Indians but also as a seat of higher learning for the youth of the colony. The Henrico project launched the first college library undertaken in British North America." On November 20, 1620, the college was given its first books which had been "sent to the Colledge in Virginia there to remaine in safftie to the use of the Collegiates hereafter, and not suffered att any time to be sent abroad, or used in the meane while."

Later in 1621, the Reverend Thomas Bargrave, rector of Henrico parish, bequeathed his sizeable library, valued at about 100 pounds, to the proposed university. With these books and finances, the endowment for the college was well underway, but the colony's catastrophe—the great Indian Massacre of 1622—virtually wiped out the town of Henrico, as well as most of the other early settlements along the James River. All the tenants on the college lands also died. Within two years, the charter of the Virginia Company was revoked and Virginia became a royal province.

Within a few years, however, the colony of Virginia began to prosper as more and more settlers came. The frontier, which hugged close along the banks of the James and other Tidewater rivers and streams, began to move back and the population grew steadily from fewer than 5,000 persons in 1635 to more than 40,000 persons in 1666. "English university graduates among the planters and within the professional classes [in Virginia] increased, strengthening public sentiment in favor of the establishment of schools and colleges," Jennings wrote. "A failure to attract an adequate supply of clergymen from England disturbed the pious, who began to direct their attention toward the possibility of founding a provincial seminary for training ministers of the gospel."

In 1660, the Virginia General Assembly en-

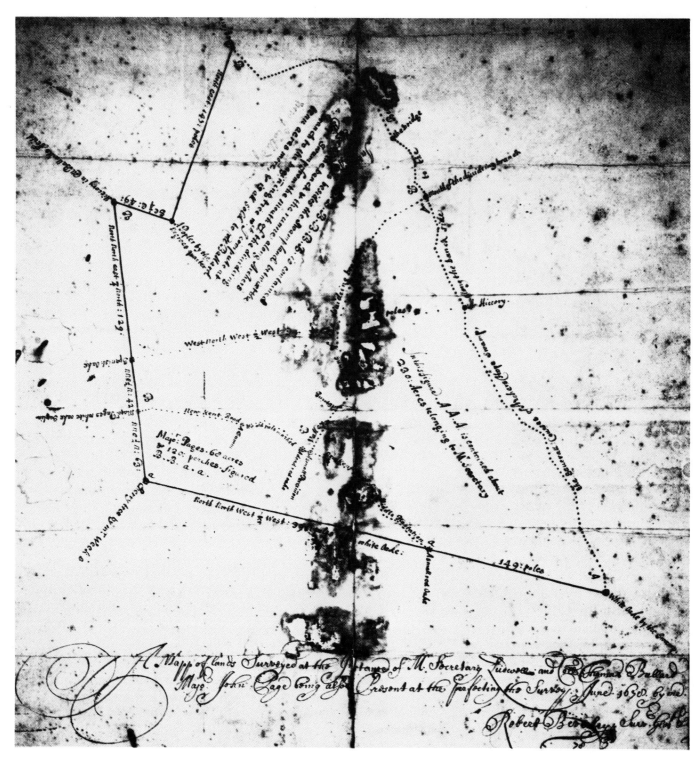

In June 1678 this survey was conducted by Robert Beverly for Thomas Ludwell, secretary of the colony of Virginia, and Colonel Thomas Ballard. Ludwell sold the land to Ballard for 110 pounds. Ballard later sold the parcel to the College of William and Mary. It encompassed 330 acres. The colonial campus is situated on this land. Courtesy of the College Archives, College of William and Mary

acted three pieces of legislation aimed at establishing a public free school and an institution, referred to as "a college of students of the liberal arts." Funds needed for the projects would be raised through personal subscriptions from the colonists. It was not, however, until 1688-89 that "a Small Remnant of Men of Better Spirit, who had either had the benefit of better Education themselves in their Mother-Country, or at least had heard of it from others" promised 2,500 pounds to endow an institution of higher education.

Blair, then rector at Jamestown, and Francis Nicholson, lieutenant-governor of the colony, became principal movers on behalf of a college. The story of Blair and the story of William and Mary are inseparable for about fifty-five years, from 1688 until his death in 1743. Blair was born in Scotland in 1655, the son of a minister of the Church of Scotland. At age eleven he entered Marischal College in Aberdeen, holding the Crombie, a scholarship in Greek, for two years. He subsequently entered the University of Edinburgh, where he received his master's degree in 1673 at age seventeen.

Apparently, the next six years were spent in diligent theological study of Presbyterianism, as evidenced through the Church of Scotland. He passed the severe "tryalls" required by the presbytery and was ordained a minister of the Church of Scotland by a bishop appointed by the king, in accordance with the dictate of James I, renewed by Charles II. Blair served for nearly three years as rector at Cranston Parish.

Those were difficult times for the Scottish clergy, with the church divided into Presbyterian and Episcopal factions. Bishops were being named and installed against the will of most Church of Scotland members. Presbyterianism, with its system of synods and presbyteries, had been retained in an abbreviated form with bishops appointed in place of the general assembly. This revival of the rule of the bishops disturbed many, but apparently not Blair, who along with other Scottish clergy favored the episcopal rule.

At the same time, the Stuart Court in England was beginning efforts in Scotland which for Blair looked very much like the reinstitution of Roman Catholicism, which he found totally unacceptable. In January 1682, he refused to sign a test oath which ultimately would place the Catholic James II as the head of the Church of Scotland when he succeeded to the English throne. Thus, at age twenty-six, Blair suddenly found himself without a career because he was ejected from his parish for refusing to sign the test oath.

As Margaret Scott Harrison wrote in her thesis, *Commissary James Blair of Virginia: A Study in Personality and Power,* Blair was a Scot of courage and conviction, with a "strong moral and uncompromising character at the same time that it added to his troubles in a world run by Englishmen." Unable to get a parish in either Scotland or England, Blair spent from 1682 to 1685 working as a secular clerk in the office of the master of rolls at London. He became acquainted with Henry Compton, the bishop of London, who also was responsible for the supervision of the Church of England beyond the seas.

"Getting missionary clergy to go to the colonies was not easy. In a land where life itself was insecure, such ministerial matters as salaries, tenure of office, and living conditions were also uncertain. The English clergymen of Virginia must have felt themselves to be in the backwaters of culture as they tried to establish church life among the people of their sprawling parishes. The rough, unsettled times worked against the orderly organization of the Church of England," Mrs. Harrison wrote. "It is to the credit of Bishop Compton and the general run of English clergy that many good men did come over in the late 17th century to serve in the church."

Blair was one of those good men whom Compton encouraged to go to the colony of Virginia as a minister. In the summer of 1685, assigned by Compton to the parish of Henrico, Blair sailed from England to the colony with twenty pounds entitlement, known as "the King's Bounty." Blair quickly settled into the life of Virginia and within two years had met and married Sarah Harrison, daughter of Col. Benjamin Harrison II.

From 1685 to 1690 Blair's parish life at Henrico was uneventful, but he was, however, learning how the church worked in its colonial field. "He was laying the groundwork for a struggle for personal power that would at one time or another in the 50 years after 1690 involve his family connections, the local church vestries, the clergy convocations, the House of Burgesses, the Governor's Council, the Royal Governors, the Privy Council, the Archbishop of Canterbury and the King himself," Mrs. Harrison wrote.

Bishop Compton was unable to travel to Virginia to supervise his clergy and examine the church's organization, so in late 1689 he decided to appoint a commissary who was to be his per-

These are English coins minted during the reign of King William III and Queen Mary II. The likenesses of the monarchs on the coins have been used throughout the college's history for illustrations. In 1968, the 275th anniversary of the founding of the College of William and Mary, the profiles were used by Professor Carl Roseberg in crafting the college's anniversary medallion for the Society of the Alumni. Courtesy of the Office of University Communications, College of William and Mary

Ralph Wormeley was one of the visitors and trustees of the College of William and Mary listed in the royal charter of February 8, 1693. He had this bookplate printed to use in his books. Courtesy of the Office of University Communications, College of William and Mary

sonal representative in Virginia. Blair was his choice and he served in the post for the next fifty-three years. Although his commission from Compton was brief, Blair understood completely the power and authority the commissary post gave him.

In 1690, the clergy convocation in Virginia petitioned the Virginia General Assembly for a college, and Blair, as commissary, pushed for its approval by the legislative body as well as the governor. Lieutenant Governor Nicholson gave the plan "all imaginable Encouragement," appointing forty-two commissioners, including Blair, to raise money for the college. In May 1691, the assembly authorized Blair to return to England with a memorial to the king and queen asking for permission to establish a college. He also carried a list of instructions and requests and a general outline for the school, structured less on the English than on Scottish universities which Blair knew firsthand.

Immediately upon arriving in England, Blair sought advice and counsel from the hierarchy of the Church of England, including Compton and other prelates: Bishop Edward Stillingfleet of Worcester, Bishop Gilbert Burnet of Salisbury, and Archbishop John Tillotson of Canterbury. Jennings noted that "the influence of these powerful churchmen, combined with the liberal disposition of the newly installed royal authorities, paved the way for Blair's success."

Archbishop Tillotson worked diligently on behalf of the college, and on November 12, 1691, Blair, accompanied by Lord Howard of Effingham, governor of the colony of Virginia, presented the memorial to the king and queen, who referred it to appropriate court officials for consideration. Tillotson told Blair that the king never took "anything better than he did the very first proposal on our college."

It was, however, the interest that Queen Mary showed in the college which raised its stock, and her endorsement proved essential. Bishop Burnet later wrote in his *History of His Own Time* that "The King had left the matters of the church wholly in the Queen's hands. He found that he could not resist importunities, which were not only vexatious to him, but had drawn preferments which he came soon to see were ill bestowed."

Bishop Burnet emphasized it was Queen Mary who continued to press for the college after the memorial was presented: "The Queen was so well pleased with the design, as apprehending the very good effects it might have, that no objection against it could move her: she hoped it might be a means of improving her own people, and of preparing some to propagate the gospel among the natives; and therefore, as she espoused the matter with a particular zeal, so the King did very readily concur with her in it."

It took fifteen months for the request to make its way through the administrative bureaucracy of Whitehall. The charter was finally granted February 8, 1693, and Blair was designated the college's first president "during his natural life." The College of William and Mary in Virginia became the second institution of higher education founded in British America.

The governance of the college was placed in the hands of a board of trustees, to become visitors when the college was fully established. Eighteen trustees were named in the royal charter, including the governor of the colony, four members of the council, nine members of the House of Burgesses and four members of the clergy. All the visitors were residents of the colony. In the charter, Blair, designated president, also was named rector for the first year, and Compton agreed to serve as the first chancellor for a term of seven years. Thereafter, in the colonial period, chancellors were selected by the visitors for a seven-year term while the rector was elected annually.

Cyprian pinx.   fecit sculp.

Chapter Two
1693-1699

In Those First Years

A s he waited in London for the acceptance of the memorial to establish a college, the Reverend James Blair was not idle. Knowing full well that a college could not be founded without adequate financial resources, the very practical Blair contacted countless persons associated with the court and the English church who could provide the needed funds.

Bishop Gilbert Burnet put him into contact with the executors of the estate of the scientist Robert Boyle, who developed the chemistry theorem known as Boyle's Law. In his will, he had left about 5,400 pounds to be invested for "pious and charitable uses." With his strong persuasive reasoning, Blair apparently had little difficulty arranging for the college to obtain some of the legacy. The executor invested the money in Brafferton Manor in Yorkshire and agreed that the college would receive the annual profits from the estate except for a bequest to Harvard College and another to the Society for the Propagation of

Sir Christopher Wren, prominent English architect and surveyor-general for King William and Queen Mary, is believed to have either designed the college's main building or approved the design developed in his office. In 1724 Hugh Jones wrote that the building "being first modelled by Sir Christopher Wren, adapted to the Nature of the Country by the Gentlemen there. . .[is] nicely contrived." Courtesy of the College Art Collection, College of William and Mary; Thomas L. Williams photo

the Gospel in New England. From the mid-1690s until the American Revolution, the college received about ninety pounds annually from the Boyle bequest.

Not wanting to neglect even the smallest opportunity, Blair made a deal with three pirates who were in jail in London. The men had plied their trade out of Virginia ports, and Blair arranged to have Edward Davies, John Hinson, and Lionel Delawafer set free with some of their booty returned to them. His reward was a gift of 300 pounds for the college.

The English government agreed that one penny tax on every pound of exported tobacco from Virginia and Maryland could be levied for the college, and additionally, the Office of Surveyor-General also was assigned to the college with its "Fees, Profits," etc. Surveyors paid for licenses. William and Mary would get the license fees, plus a percentage of the money which the surveyor would earn. Approximately 10,000 acres of land lying on the south side of Blackwater Swamp and 10,000 acres lying in an area called Pamunkey Neck, between the forks of the York River, were given to the college for its investment, on the condition that a quitrent of two copies of Latin verses be paid each year.

Also, in granting the charter, the king and queen affirmed their benevolence to the college by making an outright gift of 1,983 pounds, 14 shillings, and 10 pence from the quitrents of Virginia accumulated in the royal treasury for building and supporting the college.

In October 1693, following Blair's return to the colony, the general assembly discussed and debated the proper site for the new

A mezzotint portrait shows Henry Compton, bishop of London, who served as the first chancellor of the college from 1693 to 1700. He later served a second term from 1707 to 1713. Courtesy of the College Art Collection, College of William and Mary

This is thought to be a seventeenth century copy of the first page of a twelve-page copy of the royal charter of 1693, granted to the college by King William and Queen Mary. It is believed that this was the copy made for Sir Edmund Andros, governor of Virginia, brought to him in Jamestown by the Reverend James Blair when Blair returned from England in late 1693. Courtesy of the College Archives, College of William and Mary

On May 14, 1694, the College of Arms in London granted a coat-of-arms to the College of William and Mary. The college was the first and only American colonial college to receive a coat-of-arms. Courtesy of the Rare Books and Manuscript Department, Swem Library, College of William and Mary; Henry Grunder photo

college. Ultimately, Middle Plantation (a small community about seven miles from Jamestown, inland between the York and James rivers), was selected. The ensuing act of assembly ordered that the college should be built "as neare the church [Bruton Parish] now standing in Middle Plantation old fields as convenience will permit."

The college trustees paid Captain Thomas Ballard 170 pounds for "330 acres of land whereon ye Colledge" would be erected. In 1674 or 1675 Ballard had purchased the acres from Thomas Ludwell, secretary of the colony, for 110 pounds.

With land obtained, Blair and his trustees turned their attention to the construction of the college building. Nothing has been found in college papers or among the royal correspondence to indicate where Blair obtained the architectural drawings for the college building or who was secured as architect.

Research historian Mary R. M. Goodwin notes in her extensive research volume, *The College of William and Mary, A brief sketch of the main building,* that a surveyor for the building, Thomas Hadley, and some workmen, including bricklayers, were secured by Blair when he was in England. They later came to Virginia, bringing many of the building materials, including many paving stones. Therefore, Blair apparently considered his building plans while in London, and engaged Hadley who could have brought the plans with him to Virginia.

It was not until Hugh Jones's *The Present State of Virginia* was published in London in 1724 that Sir Christopher Wren, "Surveyor-General of the King's Works" in 1693, was associated with the main building at the college, since all the furniture, books, and records in it were destroyed in the fire of 1705. Jones wrote: "The building is beautiful and commodious, being first modelled by Sir Christopher Wren, adapted to the Nature of the Country by the Gentlemen there; and since it was burnt down, it has been rebuilt, and nicely contrived, altered and adorned by the ingenious direction of Governor Spotswood; and is not altogether unlike Chelsea Hospital."

The Reverend Jones, chaplain to the general assembly and professor of mathematics at the college, was in close contact with Blair while at the college (1716-1721), and must have obtained his information from a reliable source. He also mentioned alterations to the original plan.

The original building was to be a quadrangle, but the lack of funds forced the trustees to reduce it to an open-sided quadrangle. Mrs. Goodwin ex-
plained that if Wren or his associates, indeed, were responsible for the quadrangle design, then an earlier letter from Wren to the president of Pembroke College is illuminating. Concerning the subject of straight block buildings versus quadrangles for college living, Wren said:

"I perceive the name of a quadrangle will carry with it those whom you say may possibly be your benefactors, though it be such and the worse situation for the Chambers and the Beauty of the college... and if I had skill in enchantment to represent the pile first in one position and then in another, I should certainly make them of my opinion...But to be sober, if anybody, as you say will pay for a Quadrangle, there is no dispute to be made; let them have a Quadrangle, though a lame one, somewhat like a three legged table."

In fact, Wren did design a quadrangle for the new upper school at Eton College, erected about 1694.

Because Wren was in the employ of King William and Queen Mary, his advice almost routinely would have been sought regarding a design for the college building in Virginia. Wren also was involved in a similar situation with the bishop of London in designing the ecclesiastical buildings within the diocese of London. The construction of a college building would have required approval of Bishop Compton.

Therefore, under the system of rules of the day, the request for a building would have gone through the church commission and later through the office supervised by Wren. It also is unusual that no record of such administrative action has been uncovered, either in the multivolume papers of the Wren Society or in the Pipe Rolls (financial records of those persons employed by the crown). Furthermore, no biographers of Wren in England make any mention of the Virginia college building.

English architectural historian Marcus Whiffen, in his definitive book, *The Public Buildings of Williamsburg, An Architectural History,* acknowledges that nothing has been found in direct documentation to support that Wren or persons under his employ worked on designs for the college structure, "nor can it be held that there is anything about the building itself, as far as our knowledge of it goes, to suggest Wren's hand. Yet, when all has been said against Hugh Jones's attribution, there remains much to be said for it. The evident unsuitability of the original design for the conditions obtaining in the colony makes one the more willing to believe that it came from the

Sir Edmund Andros, governor of Virginia from 1692 to 1698, received this letter, dated April 14, 1694. It is unusual in that it is signed with the faint William R in the top left portion by King William III. The king directed Andros to give support and encouragement to the College of William and Mary. A section of the king's correspondence said, "Wee being desirous that ye Said College Should be brought to perfection, according to the true meaning & utmost Extent of Our Said Letters Patent...." Courtesy of the College Archives, College of William and Mary

A surviving boundary stone carries the date 1694 and the "W&M" cypher of King William III and Queen Mary II, similar to the cypher which the monarchs had affixed to new portions of Hampton Court, which Sir Christopher Wren renovated and rebuilt for them outside London. This photograph first appeared in Lyon G. Tyler's brief volume, The College of William and Mary in Virginia, Its History and Work, 1693-1907. The old stone now is on display in the Zollinger Museum in the Earl Gregg Swem Library. Courtesy of the College Archives, College of William and Mary

other side of the Atlantic." Blair departed England in the spring of 1693 without concluding all his college business, because we note that it was not until May of the next year that a coat of arms for William and Mary was obtained from the College of Arms.

Several interesting factors have come to light which add some favorable information for Wren proponents. English diarist John Evelyn wrote in May 1694 to a Virginian correspondent, John Walker: "Whatever else you are pleas'd to mention design'd for me will best be convey'd to me by Mr. London (his Majs Gardner here) who has an ingenious servant of his, in Virginia, not unknown I presume to you by this time; being sent thither on purpose to make and plant the Garden, designed for the new Colledge, newly built in yr country."

The Hampton Court Gardens Pipe Rolls list a James Road, gardener, and payment of 234 pounds "for going to Virginia," and he is listed as being under the employ of George London, gardener to Wren, according to Evelyn in a February 1697 diary entry. It is possible that, as a part of the Wren design, Road was to lay out a garden. Archaeological investigations on the front yard of the building have uncovered between the President's House and The Brafferton the formal garden indicated in the Bodilean copperplate, an eighteenth-century engraving depicting major Williamsburg public buildings.

Recently John Fitzhugh Millar, another architectural historian, wrote in the *William and Mary Alumni* magazine in an article on the occasion of the 350th anniversary of Wren's birth, "It is now known that Wren's younger son, William, settled in Virginia as a teenager in the 1690s (other relations already lived in Virginia) and he may well have carried any Wren plans for the college on the ship with him."

Without any discussion of possible questions raised about Wren's participation, recent biographies of King William and also of Queen Mary simply state that Wren designed or provided the design for the building. In *William's Mary*, published in 1972, Elizabeth Hamilton wrote, "The college was founded by royal charter and built to a design provided by Wren," and in *William of Orange, a personal portrait*, Nesca A. Robb wrote, "Wren provided plans for the building; a grace-ful reminder of England to set among the Virginia woods."

On August 8, 1695, a ceremony for the laying of the foundation of the College of William and Mary was held. Governor Sir Edmund Andros (who had succeeded Nicholson as governor while Blair was in England) and members of the governor's council were present. Ralph Wormley, a charter member of the college's visitors, wrote in a letter that the ceremony was conducted "with the best Solemnity" possible.

Unfortunately, work on the building went slowly and funds were lacking. Eventually it was determined that only two sides of the quadrangle could be completed in the initial construction phase. The front, or east side, was built with the north side, containing a "Great Hall."

Quarrels also arose between Governor Andros, Blair, some of the trustees and members of the council. Blair even went so far as to charge Andros with holding up construction on the college building by his actions. This would not be Blair's last encounter with a royal governor.

Prior to the building's completion, the college trustees reported in April 1697 that they had "founded a grammer school which is well furnisht with a good Schoolmaster, Usher and Writingmaster in which the schollrs make great proficiency in their studies to ye Genll satisfaction of their parents and guardians."

A special May Day program was held in 1699 sponsored by Governor Francis Nicholson, who had returned to the colony, replacing Andros. Scholars from the college made five speeches before the large gathering that included members of the council and the House of Burgesses. The third speech, probably encouraged by Nicholson, concerned the moving of the capital of the colony from Jamestown since the statehouse had recently burned. The student's remarks noted that the move to Middle Plantation would be of benefit "for the Colledge and will be a great help towards the making of a Towne, and the Towne towards the improving of the Colledge." Later that month the general assembly considered the proposal which also involved Nicholson's plans for building a capitol and surrounding city to be named Williamsburg, in honor of King William III.

The Blair Regime

The Reverend James Blair moved into the newly completed college building late in 1700, just days before the general assembly met there on December 5, 1700. With the colonial government now moved to Williamsburg, the legislature decided to meet at William and Mary until the new capital building was constructed. "The Trustees and Governours of the Colledge offer to His Excellency [Gov. Nicholson] whatsoever rooms he needs," according to the records of the executive council.

Thus, almost at once, the governor, his council, the burgesses, as well as a few Indians and the grammar master and students, moved into the building. The House of Burgesses met in the "Great Hall," and the council probably met in the large second-floor room that has come to be called the "Blue Room," where later the president and masters and the college's board of visitors met. At times during the 1700-1704 tenure of the government at the college, some of the council and college trustees

This portrait of the Reverend James Blair, first president of William and Mary, was painted in his later years and is attributed to Charles Bridges who lived in Williamsburg from 1735 to about 1745. The portrait may have been in the college's possession since Blair's presidency. The painting contains an important view of the Sir Christopher Wren Building, showing the second structure built after the fire of 1705. The phoenix symbolizes the college rising from the ashes of the fire. Courtesy of the College Art Collection, College of William and Mary; Thomas L. Williams photo

also had to lodge in the building because of insufficient accommodations in the small town.

This first main building had spacious basements and cellars which contained the kitchens, storerooms, pantries, and other housekeeping requirements. On the main floor were the grammar school and rooms for the advanced classes. The second floor contained more classrooms and rooms for the students and masters. Additional dormitory areas were located on the third floor and in the attics, but the college had never advanced beyond grammar school status when the building burned in October 1705.

As in many new structures, faults began to appear in the main building. An undated memorandum, written about 1704-1705 said, "All the chimneys in the 2n Story are scarce big enough for a Grate whereas the only firing in this Country being wood, the fire cant be made in them without running the hazard of its falling on the floor, as it once happened in the room where the Secretary's office was kept... The ovens were made within the Kitchen, but when they were heated the Smoke was so offensive that it was found necessary to pull them down and build others out of doors."

According to Blair's early outline of instruction, there were to be three levels of work: a grammar school, where Latin and Greek would be emphasized; a school of moral philosophy and a school of natural philosophy, where mathematics and sciences would be taught; and a school of divinity that would include the study of Hebrew and oriental languages, which would prepare students for the church.

It was expected that the grammar school

Swiss traveler Francis Louis Michel
drew this crude sketch of the Sir
Christopher Wren building about
1702. It is the only known depiction
of the first version of the building.
Because so little is known about that
first building, the second version of
the building, constructed between
1709 and 1716, was utilized when
the structure was restored in the late
1920s. Courtesy of the College
Archives, College of William and
Mary; Thomas L. Williams photo

Anne, the last of the Stuart monarchs,
became queen upon the death of her
brother-in-law, William III, in 1702.
Married to Prince George of Den-
mark, she was the mother of seventeen children. The principal street of
Williamsburg, Duke of Gloucester
Street, was named for one of her
sons. She died in 1714.

This eighteenth-century portrait of
Anne is from the workshop of Sir
Godfrey Kneller. The Drapers' Com-
pany of London presented it to the
college on October 13, 1961, on the
occasion of the inauguration of
William and Mary president, Davis Y.
Paschall. Courtesy of the College Art
Collection, College of William and
Mary; Thomas L. Williams photo

work would be completed by the time a young man was sixteen years old. Then he would be expected to pass an examination by the college president and masters before entering one of the two philosophical schools. Records indicate that in 1702 there were twenty-nine students in the grammar school.

Pranks have always been a part of college life, and at William and Mary they date to the early years of the school. There was an old English grammar school practice of barring the professors from their classrooms, in an effort to seek an early holiday. At Christmas 1702, some of the grammar students shut out their master and the president.

According to an account by William Robertson: "I was called out of bed to come down to Mr. Blair who I heard talking with them & persuading them to open the door, but that not succeeding he went to break it open . . . and when the negro went about breaking open the door, one of the Boys fired at him with Powder." There was no mention of shot being involved.

Robertson continued that the custom of shutting out the masters was first practiced at William and Mary in 1699 "and that the school boys had provided fire arms, but they were discovered and taken away . . . and in 1701 I heard they shutt out the Masters again."

This little incident, seemingly harmless, became a factor later in a major quarrel and personal feud between Blair and Governor Nicholson, who was also living in the building. Among the many charges which Blair made against Nicholson was that in 1702 he provided the students with money to buy powder and shot to be used during the Christmas barring out.

Mongo Ingles, headmaster of the grammar school, in a sworn affidavit, declared that "I know not the least ground for such a suggestion, having made strict enquiry amongst the scholars if they had any shot, or knew of any harm design'd against Mr. Blair." Ingles, however, had spoken against Blair and he would soon resign.

In leaving, Ingles wrote to Nicholson, saying he was quitting because he found "Mr. Blair uneasy & dissatisfied with the present Governors; & I being none of his party cannot expect to live comfortably & easy in his Society . . . [and] because he [Blair] has highly injured & disgraced not only your excellence, but my school, my Scholars & myself in one of his affidavits, by making your Excellence the contriver & my scholars the executioners of a bad design."

Ingles spared no words in predicting that "the intended College of William and Mary will never arrive at any greater Perfection than a Grammer School." About ten years later Ingles had a change of heart and accepted the post of master of the grammar school again and held it until his death.

By this time, Blair had petitioned Queen Anne asking that Nicholson be recalled, in part because of his "insolent and arbitrary methods," and his "wicked and scandalous life." So insistent was Blair that Nicholson be ousted that he returned to England and spent two years working against the governor, who finally was recalled in 1705.

On October 29, 1705, William and Mary suffered what was to become the first in a series of tragedies. The college building caught fire between 11 p.m. and midnight and "was in a small time totally consumed." The fire, apparently from a dirty chimney, set the roof ablaze near the cupola, leaving the building gutted, with only the thick walls still standing. Most of the furniture, books, and records belonging to the college were destroyed.

The general assembly was in session at the new capitol, and some members were lodging at the college. Various accounts relate that the governor and other gentlemen and townspeople, many getting up out of bed, came to see the spectacle, "but the fire had got such power before it was discovered that there was no way of putting a stop to it, and, therefore, no attempt was made to that end."

It was not until 1709 that the Trustees were able to consider rebuilding the college structure. Queen Anne had designated 500 pounds from the quit-rents for the rebuilding, and in October 1709 the college entered an agreement with John Tullitt to construct a new building for 2,000 pounds, "provided he might wood off the Colledge land and all assistants from England to come at the Colledge's risk." Blair resigned the rectorship at Jamestown that he had held since 1694 and became rector of Bruton Parish to be even nearer the college.

In June 1710, a new lieutenant governor, Alexander Spotswood, arrived in Williamsburg after five years of placid governmental activity. Spotswood immediately took an interest in the rebuilding of the college building and in its design. The trustees determined to build the new structure, using the foundation and as much of the walls as possible for the second building. The grammar school continued in facilities near the campus and by 1712 the Indian school had been estab-

A detail of the Reverend James Blair's portrait reveals the east facade of the second version of the Sir Christopher Wren Building. On October 29, 1705, a fire gutted the building. It was not until 1709, however, that the trustees could afford to rebuild the structure. The second version utilized the old walls of the first building, except on the third floor, where the walls could only be utilized in the west elevation. A roof and dormer windows had to be contrived for the east elevation. Courtesy of the College Art Collection, College of William and Mary

The great hall of the Sir Christopher Wren Building features the Queen Anne portrait above the fireplace. Queen Anne was instrumental in aiding the college following the 1705 fire. She designated 500 pounds sterling from the quitrents for the rebuilding effort. Thomas L. Williams photo

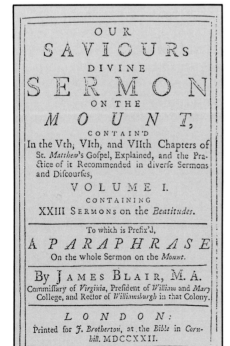

OUR
SAVIOURs
DIVINE
SERMON
ON THE
MOUNT,
CONTAIN'D
In the Vth, VIth, and VIIth Chapters of
St. *Matthew*'s Gospel, Explained, and the Pra-
ctice of it Recommended in diverse Sermons
and Discourses,
VOLUME I.
CONTAINING
XXIII SERMONS on the *Beatitudes*.

To which is Prefix'd,
A PARAPHRASE
On the whole Sermon on the *Mount*.

By JAMES BLAIR, M. A.
Commissary of *Virginia*, President of *William and Mary*
College, and Rector of *Williamsburgh* in that Colony.

LONDON:
Printed for *J. Brotherton*, at the Bible in Corn-
hill. MDCCXXII.

This is the title page of a five-volume edition of the sermons of the Reverend James Blair, published in 1722 in London. The sermons apparently were so popular that a four-volume edition was reprinted in 1740. Courtesy of the Colonial Williamsburg Foundation

lished, with about twenty Indian children attending classes.

It was Alexander Spotswood who would become the great builder of Virginia's colonial capital. Not only did he undertake to help the college, but he also completed the Governor's Palace and laid out its gardens, designed the Magazine, and was responsible for the debtors' cells added in 1711 to the Public Gaol of 1704. He also was involved in building the new church for Bruton Parish. These projects were accomplished during his twelve-year administration, which concluded with his obtaining the charter incorporating the city of Williamsburg, dated July 28, 1722.

In describing the second college building, Whiffen wrote, "... the west wall of the main range was probably little damaged by the fire and retained *in toto*. The other walls of the main range were pulled down or built up, as their condition demanded, to approximately the level of the third floor. The third storey, which in the first building was enclosed by walls on all four sides, could therefore be enclosed in the roof and lighted by dormer windows on all sides but the west, where it was lighted by the windows in the original west wall." It was probably Spotswood, the amateur architect, who suggested building the third floor in that fashion to save money. By 1716 construction had been virtually completed on the building.

The College of William and Mary began to break out of the grammar school mold with the appointment, recommended by Spotswood, of the Reverend Tanaquil Lefevre as professor of mathematics and natural philosophy on April 25, 1711, but he was dismissed on January 28, 1712. Later the Reverend Hugh Jones was appointed in 1717 as professor of mathematics. Students came to the school in increasing numbers, many from the great plantations. Young Benjamin Harrison came from Berkeley Hundred, Carter Page from Rosewell, and Edward Randolph from Turkey Island. Although there were only two or three professors, the college still had two parts—a philosophy school, roughly the undergraduate program, and a divinity school, which conducted graduate work.

Amid all the activity Blair was still the driving force for William and Mary, doing battle with one and all who stood in his way, fighting to gain personal power or against those who would destroy his college. His fights with royal governors were legendary and have been detailed in numerous accounts.

He also fought with masters at the college as well as the other clergy in Virginia. In 1719, at the annual clergy convention, Jones, who a year earlier had been chaplain to the House of Burgesses, led the opposition to Commissary Blair, which naturally strained their relations on campus. Jones resigned his college appointment and returned to England in 1721. His book, *The Present State of Virginia,* was published three years later. In the book's appendix, Jones presented suggestions for the improvement of the college, noting that it was:

"... Now a College without a Chapel, without a Scholarship and without a statute.... There is a library without books, comparatively speaking.... There have been Disputes and Differences about these and the like... of the College without end.... These things greatly impede the Progress of Sciences and learned Arts."

His criticism also included the students, who, he felt, were "for the most part desirous only of learning what is absolutely necessary, in the shortest and best Method.... Another thing prejudicial to the College, is the Liberty allowed the Scholars, and the negligent Observance of College Hours, and the opportunity they have to rambling Abroad."

This fragment is the only remaining evidence of the 1717 bell that hung for years in the cupola of the Sir Christopher Wren Building. The bell was apparently ordered in 1716 and hung until it was destroyed in the fire of 1859. Courtesy of the College Archives, College of William and Mary

Chapter Four
1697-1743

The Indians and Blair's House

I n his settlement of 1697 with the Earl of Burlington, nephew and executor of the estate of Robert Boyle, Blair agreed that the president and masters of William and Mary were to "keep att the said Colledge soe many Indian Children in Sicknesse and health in Meat, drink, Washing, Lodgeing, Cloathes, Medicines, books and Educacon from the first beginning of Letters till they are ready to receive Orders and be thought Sufficient to be sent abroad to preach and Convert the Indians at the rate of fourteen pounds per Annum for every such Child."

It is unclear when the Indian school at the college was established, but some records point to about 1700 when Lieutenant Governor Nicholson gave instructions to west-bound traders that they should tell the Indians "that a great & good man who lately died in England...having a great love for the Indians, hath left money enough to the College here in Virginia to keep 9 or 10 Indian children at it, & to teach them to read, write & all other arts &

The Honorable Robert Boyle (1627-1691), philosopher and scientist, is depicted in this eighteenth-century portrait. Funds from his estate were used to construct The Brafferton. Other Boyle funds were used directly to support the Indians' education. The painting, by James Worsdale, was one of the earliest gifts of art to the college, received in 1732 from Boyle's nephew Lord Burlington and first hung in the second-floor library of the building. Courtesy of the College Art Collection, College of William and Mary; Thomas L. Williams photo

sciences, that the best Englishmen's sons do learn," and that their rooms would be ready for them the following summer.

Nicholson suggested that the boys be seven or eight years of age and he invited the chiefs themselves to visit the college. There are no records of how many Indians were enrolled. In the early 1700s, however, the college began the practice of buying its pupils from local Indians who captured the young boys during wars with distant tribes. Christopher Jackson taught four or five Indians prior to 1710.

Later, Alexander Spotswood also wanted to foster a thriving Indian school. By 1712, he managed to overcome much of the distrust among local chiefs, who finally consented to allow their young boys to attend the white man's school, "as hostages for their Fidelity." About twenty young Indians were enrolled, including the son of a Pamunkey chief, the son and cousin of the chief of the Nottoways, and two sons of the chief rulers of the Meherrin Indians. After the fire of 1705, they apparently were taught in a schoolhouse near the college until the building was rebuilt.

Having so many Indians, however, taxed the college's funds, and Governor Spotswood had to turn to the House of Burgesses for additional support. The burgesses failed to share the governor's enthusiasm and his request was turned down. The disappointed governor wrote: "I cannot but be extremely concerned to find this design slighted by the House of Burgesses, and so violent an humor prevail amonst them for extirpating all the Indians without distinction of friends or enemys." It was a shattering blow to the school and enrollment dropped immediately. By 1721

Chelsea Hospital in London is portrayed in this detail from an eighteenth-century engraving. Hugh Jones, a former William and Mary professor who had returned to London, wrote in 1724 that the main college building "is not altogether unlike Chelsea Hospital." Like the hospital, the college when completed had twin wings, with a great hall in one wing and a chapel in the other. Sir Christopher Wren, who is believed to have designed the original college building, also designed the hospital. Courtesy of the Colonial Williamsburg Foundation

This is the title page from the pamphlet on the Charter and Statutes of the College of William and Mary in Virginia that William Parks, editor of the Virginia Gazette, published in 1736. It was the first American publication of the charter. Courtesy of the College Archives, College of William and Mary

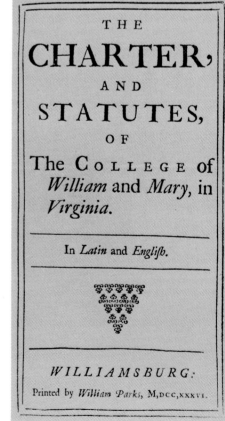

THE

CHARTER,

AND

STATUTES,

OF

The COLLEGE of *William* and *Mary*, in *Virginia*.

In *Latin* and *English*.

WILLIAMSBURG:

Printed by *William Parks*, M,DCC,XXXVI.

there was not a single Indian at William and Mary.

In 1718, the Virginia General Assembly did pass an act to give 1,000 pounds for the scholarship fund "for educating ingenious scholars, natives of this colony," but apparently this was not for Indian "natives."

Blair used money from the Brafferton estate, apparently accumulated through the years because so few Indians had attended the school, to build a building at the campus to serve as the Indian school, housing the Indians' schoolmaster and his pupils. In 1723, the structure was constructed in the front yard of the main building and was called The Brafferton, after the English estate from which the funding came.

The Brafferton was constructed, after the fashion of the period, of Virginia brick with glazed headers laid in Flemish bond. It was three stories high including the attic with its dormer windows. Henry Cary, the younger, was probably the builder, since he took over the construction of the Governor's Palace three years earlier and built the house for President Blair on campus nine years later.

The building was designed for three large rooms to a floor, on the two principal floors, with one large room to the west and two smaller rooms to the east of a central hallway. It is believed that initially the third floor was not divided, but was partitioned sometime before 1736 to provide more accommodations for the Indians.

How the rooms were used for the Indian school is not known. It appears that the master of the school had the two smaller rooms downstairs and the larger room was the classroom. On the second floor over the schoolroom was a library, for which Lord Burlington sent Robert Boyle's portrait. Until the Revolution, the Boyle estate continued to provide funds for the college and its Indians, "although most of them seemed to have forgotten their prayers and catechism when they left Williamsburg," one Virginian later observed.

In 1728 Colonel William Byrd wrote of the Indians: "And here I must lament the bad success Mr. Boyle's charity has hitherto had towards converting any of these poor heathens to Christianity. Many children of our neighboring Indians have been brought up in the College of William and Mary. They have been taught to read and write, and have been carefully instructed in the principles of the Christian religion, till they came to be men. Yet after they returned home, instead of civilizing and converting the rest, they immediately relapsed into infidelity and barbarism themselves."

Masters, as well as Indians, came and went during most of the history of the Indian school. Those Indians who did stay at the college were plagued with homesickness and loneliness and proved highly susceptible to the white man's illnesses and to the white man's alcohol.

The idea of educating an Indian boy in the white man's manners and then placing him back into his own culture may have sounded like progressive thinking on the part of charitable colonists, but the plan simply did not work. The tribal chiefs became very reluctant to send boys to the school. One chief reportedly declined an offer to send his boys, saying, "When they came back to us, they were bad runners, ignorant of every means of living in the wood, unable to bear either cold or hunger...were therefore neither fit for hunters, warriors, nor councilors; they were totally good for nothing."

Another of the reasons for the school was an effort to bring the Indians and colonists closer together. Unfortunately, the experiences of one of the school's last pupils, a half-breed named Baubee, demonstrated the school often had the opposite effect.

Brought to William and Mary in 1773, Baubee attended the classes for several years, but when he returned to his tribe he spread bitter reports about the unkind treatment he received at the school. He also used the benefits of his education in an attempt to persuade the Indians to go to war against the whites.

Whether he was trying to get funds to support the Indian school, or other activities of the college, money was a constant problem for Blair. He was lucky enough to secure additional sums along the way from the general assembly, such as in 1726 when 200 pounds per year was allocated from duties paid on imported spirits for twenty-one years. The crown later affirmed the assembly's action, which was amended in 1736 to give the college a penny-per-gallon tax on all such imports.

Blair journeyed to England in 1726-1727 to obtain approval of the act of 1726 concerning those 200 pounds a year which was being contested by Francis Nicholson in London, to obtain the first college statute, and to arrange the transfer of the college. He joined the surviving trustee, the Reverend Stephen Fouace, a clergyman who had been in the colony in 1693, but returned home to England early in the 1700s. Blair and Fouace, with the advice of then chancellor Dr. William Wake,

Between 1734 and 1776, funds secured by William and Mary from the provincial levy on wines and liquors were used to purchase volumes for the college library. Bookplates, like this one surviving in a volume, were affixed to all such books. Courtesy of the College Archives, College of William and Mary; Thomas L. Williams photo

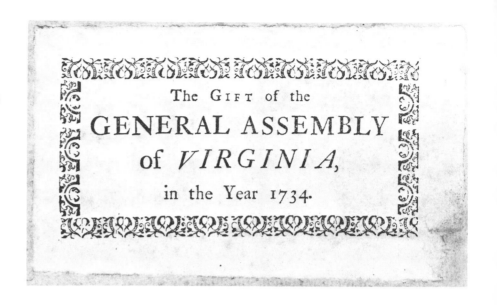

The GIFT of the
GENERAL ASSEMBLY
of *VIRGINIA*,
in the Year 1734.

This sterling silver two-handled communion cup, now called the Lady Gooch Cup, was bequeathed to the college in 1775 by Lady Rebecca Gooch, the wife of the English royal Lieutenant Governor William Gooch. It was given in memory of her son, who had been a student at William and Mary. Courtesy of the College Art Collection, College of William and Mary

In a segment of the surviving minutes of the William and Mary faculty is this oath, in Latin. All professors at the college were required to sign the oath of conformity to the Church of England. It was placed in the minutes on January 26, 1738, and signed by a number of professors until 1771. Courtesy of the College Archives, College of William and Mary

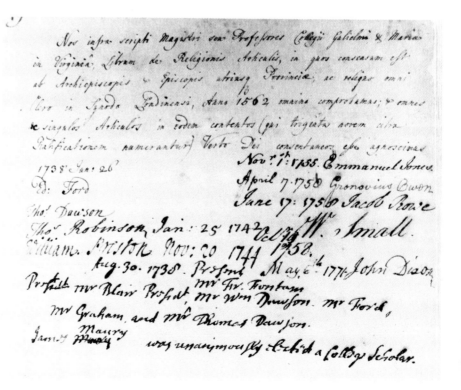

archbishop of Canterbury, prepared the first "statutes" for the college later in 1727. There were certain requirements for a president: "a man of Gravity, that is in Holy Orders, of an unblemished Life, a good reputation and not under Thirty Years of Age."

The statutes also outlined the requirements of the several schools within the college, vested ordinary government in the president and masters or professors, and declared "reserving notwithstanding the Power given by the Charter to the Visitors and Governors of the said college, namely, that proceeding regularly, they may even change these, as their Affairs and Circumstances may from Time to Time require."

The purposes of the college also were defined in the statutes: "The Youth of Virginia should be well educated to Learning and good Morals; the Churches of America, especially *Virginia,* should be supplied with good Ministers after the Doctrine and Government of the Church of *England;* [and] the *Indians* of *America* should be instructed in the Christian Religion and that some of the *Indian* Youth . . . be sent out to preach the Gospel to their Countrymen in their own Tongue." *The Charter and Statutes of The College of William and Mary in Virginia* were first printed in Williamsburg, in both Latin and English, in 1736 by William Parks, editor of *The Virginia Gazette.*

By 1729 there were finally enough revenues for President Blair to employ a full complement of six masters or professors—the Reverend William Dawson and Alexander Irwin of the philosophical school; the Reverend Bartholomew Yates and the Reverend Francis Fontaine of the divinity school; Joshua Fry, master of the grammar school, and Richard Cocke, master of the Indian school. With all ranks filled, as required by the royal charter, the surviving trustees—Blair and Fouace—took action to transfer the College of William and Mary to the president and masters of the school. The trustees called upon King George II to transfer the college "and all houses, edifices and buildings, courts, gardens and orchards thereunto belonging, to have and to hold all and singular . . . unto the said President and masters, or professors of the College . . . and their successors for ever."

There also was enough money on hand for the college to construct the third side of the quadrangle of the main building. The south, or chapel wing, was completed and dedicated on June 28, 1732. It is also believed that Blair about this time envisioned a building similar to The Brafferton, across the college yard, for use as a president's house. Naturally, it would be less expensive than completing the fourth side of the quadrangle.

A month later, on July 31, the foundations of the President's House were laid with Henry Cary, Jr., as its builder. He was the grandson of Miles Cary, one of the trustees named in the royal charter. One of the few surviving scattered entries from the colonial faculty minutes, mentions "The President, Mr Dawson, Mr Fry, Mr Stith and Mr Fox, laying the first five bricks in order, one after another."

The President's House, though almost identical to The Brafferton, was four feet larger in each dimension. The house also had various outbuildings, including a kitchen with rooms above it, a laundry, a wellhead, and a "necessary house." There was a fruit and vegetable garden to the west. There were no brick walls around college property until the twentieth century, but there were fences and by 1776 a fence was put around the president's yard.

Before the President's House was built, Blair and his wife apparently had an apartment in the main building. It is known, however, that he owned a house and plantation in James City County within two miles of the college, part of Rich Neck plantation.

Blair's sermons, about 117 preached either at Jamestown or Williamsburg between 1707 and 1721, were published in London in five volumes in 1722 and were considered good enough to be reprinted in 1740 in a four-volume edition.

James Blair, a member of the governor's council except for two brief suspensions, attended his last council meeting at the capitol on March 29, 1743, and he died at the President's House on April 18, 1743, in the fiftieth year of his presidency. He left 500 pounds for a scholarship in the divinity school and all of his books to the college. Lieutenant Governor William Gooch, in a letter to his brother, Thomas, bishop of Norwich, wrote, "Old Blair died last moneth in his 88th Year . . . . If his Belly had been as sound as his Head and Breast, he might have lived many years longer."

Chapter Five
1743-1776
Jefferson and the Coming Revolution

ith the death of James Blair in 1743, an important epoch in the life of the College of William and Mary ended. The great power and influence which the commissary wielded throughout his fifty-year presidency insured the college's survival. Blair had not only been president of the college, but had served as commissary of the bishop of London, as a member of the governor's council and at one time as acting governor of the colony.

The new president was the Reverend William Dawson, who had been at the college since 1729 when he was named professor of moral philosophy. He was a graduate of Queens College, Oxford, with both bachelor's and master's degrees. Archbishop William Wake of Canterbury, then chancellor of William and Mary, had recommended him as a faculty member.

John Jennings, in his volume on the college library, stresses that most of the faculty at the school between 1729 and 1757 were alumni of Queens. "Symbolic of the relationship was the dramatic appearance of President William Dawson and three of his full professors in complete Queens academic regalia on the occasion of the formal celebration of Transfer Day (when the college in 1729 was transferred from the trustees to the president and masters) in 1747," Jennings wrote. The link with Queens College accentuated scholarship, stressed the need for improving library resources, and put "a new emphasis on classical studies at the college."

Dawson seemed to be popular from the time of his arrival at the school and became friends with many of the colony's most influential men, including Lieutenant Governor William Gooch and Sir John Randolph. Early in his tenure at the college Dawson had served as chaplain to the house of burgesses, and assisted Blair at Bruton Parish. He was given his own parish at Jamestown in 1741.

On his deathbed, Blair told Dawson that he did not doubt he "would be chosen President... (and) earnestly recommended to him to be carefull of the Youth at the College that they might be well instructed in Doctrines of the Church of England," a college document stated. Dawson also succeeded Blair as commissary.

Continuing as moral philosophy professor for a year, until he was replaced, Dawson worked diligently to make the school prosper. Records of this period are very scarce, but the surviving documents indicate that he had well-recommended masters and professors. Governor Gooch encouraged Dawson at every turn and assisted him in gaining additional stature in the colony by having him appointed to the

There is no known portrait of Thomas Jefferson in his youth. Noted Richmond artist David Silvette, however, studied every likeness of Jefferson and produced this rendering in 1975. Jefferson was a student and boarded in the Sir Christopher Wren Building between 1760 and 1762. In 1779, as governor of Virginia, he proposed a reorganization plan which made William and Mary the nation's first university. Courtesy of the University of Virginia

council. Gooch later pushed for Queens College to grant Dawson a doctor of divinity degree, saying the degree certainly had been earned in Virginia and would be advantageous to him "in the Exercise of Ecclesiastical authority."

The degree was finally obtained, without Dawson having to return to England to take his oath and receive the diploma, which, along with his regalia, reached him in August 1747. On January 30, 1747, the capitol burned and the general assembly again was housed in the main college building until the new capitol was ready in 1753. The relationship between Dawson and Gooch was strengthened for the benefit of the college. Gooch, however, returned to England in 1750 and Dawson died in 1752.

Since its beginning, the college had been designated as the institution to issue surveyors' licenses for the colony. Seventeen-year-old George Washington obtained a license from the college and on July 29, 1747, appeared before the Culpeper County court with a commission appointing him surveyor of the county. It was Washington's first public office, obtained under the auspices of William and Mary.

An event in November 1750 saw the formation of the F.H.C. Society, the first student secret society in America, and probably the first college fraternity in British America. In her lively account, *James Innes and His Brothers of the F.H.C.,* Dr. Jane Carson explained that the organization was active in the 1770s, but, like other groups, lapsed during the Revolutionary War. Unlike the Greek-letter fraternities of a later date, it established no branches at other American colleges and was not revived until the nineteenth century.

Members always called it the F.H.C. Society, never divulging the secret of the Latin words represented by the letters, but they specifically mentioned their devotion to friendship, mirth and conviviality, science and charity. In the late nineteenth and in the twentieth century, it has been called popularly the "Flat Hat Club." The names of the original members are not known. However, in the early 1770s the members included James Innes, St. George Tucker, Beverly Randolph, Thomas Davis, Walker Maury, Robert Baylor, and William Yates.

Thomas Jefferson became a member during his years of study, 1760-1762. Jefferson, writing in 1819, said, "When I was a student of Wm & Mary College . . . there existed a society called the F.H.C. Society, confined to the number of six students

only, of which I was a member, but it had no useful object, nor do I know whether it now exists."

One of the "useful objects" which Jefferson probably forgot was the society's goal in the years prior to the Revolution to help secure volumes for its library. A list was compiled and some books secured. It is not known how many books were eventually purchased because only one F.H.C. book now survives: a 1775 volume of *A System of Moral Philosophy,* written by Francis Hutcheson, professor of philosophy at the University of Glasgow. The other volumes apparently burned in later college fires.

Many persons in the colony hoped that William Dawson's brother Thomas, a senior master at the college, would succeed him as president. The new president, however, was the Reverend William Stith, a distinguished historian, a former master of the grammar school, and William Dawson's brother-in-law. He was elected by a close vote and his administration was a brief, rather uneventful one.

Stith died September 19, 1755 and immediately was succeeded by the Reverend Thomas

An engraving plate, circa 1740, was found in December 1929, in the Bodleian Library, Oxford, England; it showed the front campus of the college (top row), and the rear elevation of the Wren building, with its two wings (center, second row). Also pictured is the colonial capitol building (left, second row) and the Governor's Palace (right, second row). The original copperplate engraving was presented to John D. Rockefeller, Jr., in 1937, and is now owned by the Colonial Williamsburg Foundation. Courtesy of the Colonial Williamsburg Foundation; Thomas L. Williams photo

This bond, signed on September 18, 1749, bound George Currie and Richard Bland of Prince George County to the college in the sum of 100 pounds. It is not known what the document means or when the money was eventually collected. Richard Bland was one of Virginia's colonial patriots. In 1960, when a two-year college was established in Prince George County, near Petersburg, it was named for him. The school still functions under the William and Mary board of visitors. Courtesy of the College Archives, College of William and Mary

KNOW all Men by these Presents, That We George Currie & Richard Bland both of the County of Prince George Gent. are held and firmly bound unto the President, and Masters of the College of William and Mary, in Virginia, in the Sum of one Hundred Pounds Sterling ; to be paid unto the said President, and Masters, their Successors, or Attorney : To the Paiment whereof, well and truly to be made, We bind our selves, and each of us, our, and each of our Heirs, Executors, and Administrators, jointly and severally, firmly, by these Presents. Sealed with our Seals, and dated this Eighteenth — — — Day of September in the Year of our Lord, One Thousand Seven Hundred and Forty Nine

On November 11, 1750, the first student secret society in America, and probably the first college fraternity in British America, was founded at William and Mary. It was called the F.H.C., but its members never divulged what Latin words the letters represented. The organization has been revived several times at the college. In the late nineteenth and twentieth centuries other students simply called it the "Flat Hat Club." Courtesy of the College Archives, College of William and Mary

Dawson, who earlier had been made commissary. Also a member of the council and rector of Bruton Parish Church, he united all the posts held earlier by Blair. His presidency was rife with dissentions and discontent, not only because of the French and Indian War, but also because of the wrangling in the colony, church, and college.

At the time of his appointment, Dawson was master of the Indian school, where eight Indians were enrolled in 1754-1755; other students at the college numbered only sixty-seven in 1754 and fifty-five in 1755. On April 20, 1756, Dawson and the masters and professors of the college conferred the first honorary degree, a master of arts, upon Benjamin Franklin. In a letter to his wife, Franklin wrote, "Virginia is a pleasant Country, now in full Spring; the People extremely obliging and polite."

The masters and professors were fighting with the visitors for power, a battle which continued for another twenty years. Dawson was caught in the middle. The president and masters expelled two grammar school students and removed an usher (assistant teacher), but the visitors entered the picture by dismissing the Reverend Thomas Robinson, master in the grammar school for fifteen years. The visitors then questioned the removal of the usher. The masters challenged the visitors' authority, and three masters—the Reverend John Camm, the Reverend Richard Graham, and the Reverend Emmanuel Jones—were subsequently removed by the visitors. The masters, however, refused to "deliver up the Keys to their Schools, & Apartments" and Mr. Graham refused to deliver "the Seal, & Papers belonging to the College." Later Dawson, following the visitors' directives, put new locks on the doors.

A much later commissary, the Reverend William Robinson of Stratton-Major Parish, King and Queen County, wrote to Bishop Terrick of London strongly criticizing the visitors; and in 1763 the privy council in England "reinstated in their Places" Camm and Graham. At the request of the visitors, replacements were sent from England. Governor Dinwiddie wrote to his friend, after his return to England: "...Pray to not let your good nature allow them [the new professors] too much familiarity but keep them to their duties...[and hopefully this change in faculty would] relieve the Character of the College & engage the Gentlemen to send their children to it as formerly."

In 1758, the Reverend Goronwy Owen was named grammar school master. A graduate of Jesus College, Oxford, Owen was the "premier

Praeses et Magistri Collegii GULIELMI et MARIAE in Virginia.

Omnibus ad quos hoc praesens Scriptum pervenerit, Salutem in Domino sempiternam.

Quum in Chartâ sua regiâ nobis concessum et confirmatum sit, ut eos, qui se literis et studiis inter praecipue ornarunt, Gradibus academicis decoremus; Quum volumus hujusmodi Honorem imprimis civibus indignissimum, quae nobis et Juventuti Virginiensi Exemplum, regium proponamus, Quumq. Benjaminum Franklin ... Americanis in eam collatus; quaedam Honores a Rege Christianissimo rea Scientiarum apud ... Academiâ, a regiâ Societate Londinensi et accumulati, nec non ejusdem Celebritas et gloria, et minis in Philosophia naturali Praefectiones excogitatas, per totam Literarum Rempublicam evulgata. Idcirco in frequenti Senatu Die secundo Mensis Aprilis Anno Domini MDCCLVI habito, conspirantibus omnibus Suffragiis, praefatum Benjaminum Franklin Armigerum, Virum omni Laude dignum, Artium Magistrum renunciavimus et constituimus. In cujus Rei Testimonium huic Diplomati Sigillum Collegii Gulielmi et Mariae commune apponi fecimus. — Dat. Die Non. et An. praedict:

This is the honorary degree presented to Benjamin Franklin by the college in 1756. On this document the seal and the signatures of the faculty and president are missing. Courtesy of the American Philosophical Society

Benjamin Franklin, printer, scientist, and later one of the signers of the Declaration of Independence, was the first person to receive an honorary degree from the college. He received a master of arts degree on April 2, 1756. This mezzotint portrait was by Edward Savage after David Martin. Courtesy of the National Portrait Gallery, Smithsonian Institution, Washington, D.C.

47

George Washington appeared before the Culpeper County court on July 29, 1747, with a commission appointing him surveyor of the county. He had received his surveyor's license at age seventeen from William and Mary, which had been granted authority to issue such licenses for the colony of Virginia. It was Washington's first public office. Courtesy of Washington and Lee University

This is a portion of a page from the bursar's book recording the attendance at William and Mary of Thomas Jefferson from Albemarle County. He was not yet seventeen years old when he entered the college. The record indicates that he came to the school on March 25, 1760, and left April 25, 1762. His total fees for room and board were 27 pounds, 1 shilling, 8 pence. Jefferson later wrote the Declaration of Independence, was the third president of the United States, and founded the University of Virginia. Courtesy of the College Archives, College of William and Mary

poet" of Wales and a man of great learning, but he was removed in 1760 because of his overfondness for the wine cup. Dawson became embroiled in Owen's departure and found himself later being accused of drunkenness. His spirit broken, Dawson died in November 1760, just months after William and Mary's most illustrious alumnus came to campus.

Thomas Jefferson arrived at William and Mary on March 25, 1760. The college had just weathered an internal political storm and its faculty was reduced by half, to three, with enrollment numbering perhaps one hundred. Two-thirds of the students, including Jefferson, lodged and boarded at the college.

According to Jefferson's biographer, Dumas Malone, "as the term 'gentleman' was understood in 18th century Virginia, Thomas Jefferson was one by reason of birth, landed estate, and training." Not quite seventeen years old, the youth from Albemarle County had already been trained in Latin, Greek, and geology by backcountry tutors. There were two principal professors in the philosophy school, and, as Malone wrote, "there was nothing institutional about this species of education; it was intimate and personal and its success naturally depended on the quality of the persons."

William Small, professor of natural philosophy (science and mathematics) took over the area of moral philosophy (ethics, rhetoric, and belles lettres) a few months after Jefferson arrived. "During most of his stay in college Small was the only teacher he had . . . to all practical purposes he was tutored by Small, who, outside the classroom, made an intellectual companion of this eager and promising lad from the hills," Malone explained.

Later Jefferson said of Small, his inspiring teacher: "It was my great fortune, and what probably fixed the destinies of my life that Dr. William Small of Scotland was then professor of mathematics [at the college], a man profound in most of the useful branches of science, with a happy talent of communications, correct and gentlemanly manners and an enlarged and liberal mind."

Small was a minor torchbearer of the Enlightenment, which Sir Isaac Newton and John Locke had kindled. Malone wrote, "Jefferson, in the bright springtime of his life and this bright springtime of the modern mind, plunged into this endlessly fascinating physical world (as presented by Small) with an enthusiasm and curiosity which never lessened, gaining distinction in numerous fields from architecture, writing, politics to botany and meteorology."

The college course in Jefferson's day consisted of four years of study in the philosophy school and contained a rigorous study schedule from 7:00 to 11:00 a.m. and from 2:00 to 6:00 p.m. and Jefferson studied about fifteen hours per day. After completing his work at William and Mary on April 25, 1762, Jefferson commuted between Williamsburg and Albemarle for several years while studying law in the office of George Wythe. Jefferson wrote later that he revered Wythe above Small as "my earliest and best friend . . . to him I am indebted for first impressions which have had the most salutary influence on the course of my life."

Wythe, who Jefferson called his "beloved mentor," taught him all the law of the day. Malone wrote that the study of law "evoked from Jefferson no such enthusiasms as forays into classical literature or scientific explorations, but he did not dislike the subject. He found any form of intellectual activity challenging and rewarding." By the time he concluded his studies with Wythe, Jefferson was twenty-two or twenty-four years old and had a highly trained and well-ordered mind. He had acquired an education which anybody in any age might envy. In 1767 Jefferson was admitted to the bar and began to practice law immediately.

Jefferson did not like Georgian architecture and described the college building and nearby Public Hospital as "rude, mis-shapen piles, which but that they have roofs, would be taken for brick kilns." In a fit of romantic gloom he referred to the town several times as "Devilsburg."

Midway through Jefferson's stay at the college, in 1761, the Reverend William Yates was named president, succeeding Dawson. He was the first native-born American and the first of several William and Mary alumni to hold the post. Yates's administration was relatively uneventful. The college did adopt certain rules for "discretionary punishment" for scholars "of what Age, Rank, or Quality soever," and decided that each master could inflict the punishment he deemed appropriate on a student "behaving in an indecent and irregular Manner."

Yates died on October 5, 1764, and the Reverend James Horrocks, graduate of Trinity College, Cambridge, and grammar school master since 1762, became president and rector of Bruton Parish, later securing the posts of commissary and membership on the governor's council. He was selected over the Reverend Richard Graham, the

Cherokee Indian chief, Austenaco (center), from western Virginia, visited Williamsburg in 1765 and was a guest of the college president, Reverend James Horrocks, in the President's House. The chief came to appeal the decision of the colonial government to move his tribe from the Virginia mountains to new lands in western North Carolina. Courtesy of the Colonial Williamsburg Foundation

A twentieth-century lithograph portrait of Lord Botetourt, governor of Virginia from 1768 to 1770, was given to the college by the artist Albert Rosenthal. Courtesy of the College Art Collection, College of William and Mary; Thomas L. Williams photo

Just before his death, Lord Botetourt, governor of Virginia and rector of the college, gave the college funds to establish two gold medals. They were to be given to the best scholar in the classics and the best scholar in philosophy. Eight gold medals were struck in England and awarded from 1772 to 1775. The obverse is the head of King George III, and the reverse is King William III and Queen Mary II granting the charter to the kneeling Reverend James Blair. In 1941 the college reestablished the award and new dies were prepared from an existing gold medal. One Botetourt Medal is now annually awarded to the graduating student who has achieved the highest scholarship record over four years. Courtesy of the College Archives, College of William and Mary; Thomas L. Williams photo

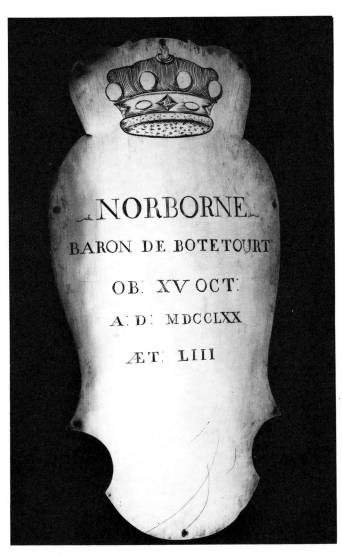

This silver coffin plate from the coffin of Norborne Berkeley, baron de Botetourt, was crafted in Williamsburg in 1770 by William Waddill. The plate was stolen from the crypt under the Sir Christopher Wren Building, presumably during the Civil War, and returned to the college in 1889 by E. P. Bevillard, a Rome, New York jeweler to whom it had been sold as scrap. Courtesy of the College Art Collection, College of William and Mary

senior master or professor. His tenure was replete with strife.

The visitors passed more statutes, one of which forbade the professors to take charge of churches in the vicinity of the college. The visitors gave themselves the power to remove professors "at pleasure," and to exercise direct control over the college's finances. The professors charged these were powers not defined in the charter and appealed to the bishop of London. Camm, who had returned to the faculty as professor of divinity, and the Reverend Josiah Johnson, master of the grammar school, moved into the town when they each married. (College rules did not allow professors to be married.) The visitors threatened to remove them, but a compromise resulted. After 1769 any future professor who married would immediately forfeit his professorship.

In 1768, Norborne Berkeley, baron de Botetourt, became royal governor of Virginia and a member of the college board of visitors, later serving as rector. In 1770, just prior to his untimely death, he gave the college funds to establish two gold medals, to be given to the best scholar in the classics and the best in philosophy. The number of students at the college was about 120, with about 85 boarding in the main building. There were about seventy students in the Grammar School and Indian School and about fifty scholars in the philosophy school.

The visitors, by statute passed in 1770, made the first substantial changes in curriculum, eliminating the rules requiring training in Latin and Greek in the grammar school, prior to studying in the philosophical school. "All such Youth, whether resident in or out of the college, who had acquired a competent Knowledge of common or vulgar Arithmetic, & whose Parents or Guardians may desire it, be received into the Mathematical School," the revision read.

In 1771, Horrocks, with the support of Camm, who had been reinstated by the privy council in England as professor of divinity, initiated a fresh upheaval. They called a convention of the clergy to consider the question of an American episcopate—a bishop for the church in the colonies—but only ten clergy attended and opposition was vigorous. In June 1771, Horrocks sailed for England. There is little information of his activities while in England. He died enroute home at Oporto, Portugal, March 20, 1772. Camm, the last of the colonial presidents, succeeded him.

The visitors decided in 1772 "to make an

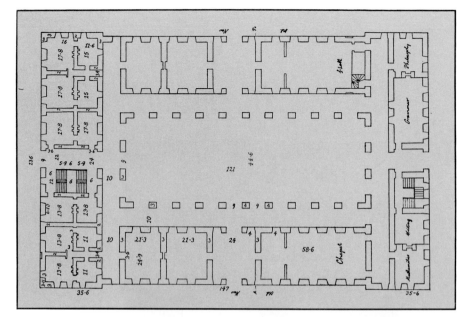

John Murray, earl of Dunmore, the last royal governor of Virginia, and a member of the college's board of visitors, asked Thomas Jefferson to design a plan for an addition to the college's main building. Initially, the building was to have been built as a quadrangle, but only three of the sides were constructed. In Jefferson's plan of 1772, the size of the Sir Christopher Wren Building would have been doubled. The original building with its chapel and great hall are at the bottom of the drawing. The building proposed by Jefferson is at the top. Courtesy of the Massachusetts Historical Society; Colonial Williamsburg Foundation photo

additional building to the College," and lodged a plan for the work with Matthew Davenport, a tavern keeper in Williamsburg, requesting estimates before October 1772. John Murray, the earl of Dunmore and last royal governor, was a member of the visitors and asked Jefferson to draw up a plan for the addition. The purpose was to double the size of the building and complete the quadrangle, as originally proposed in 1695.

Work on the addition was started and foundations were laid behind the main building, but the project was discontinued at the outbreak of the Revolution. During this turbulent period, James Monroe, who later would serve as the fifth president of the United States, attended the college from 1774-1776.

On April 3, 1775, Dunmore announced his intention to resign as a visitor, and seventeen days later the governor ordered the removal of the gunpowder from the magazine in the city, which started active revolutionary confrontations in Williamsburg.

In June 1775, the Reverend Samuel Henley and the Reverend Thomas Gwatkins, professors with strong Tory leanings, returned to England with Lady Dunmore and her children. Camm, a councilor and friend of Dunmore, sided with the governor as the quarrel between the colonies and the mother country accelerated.

In September 1775, Colonel Patrick Henry established a campground at the rear of the college for Virginia troops who were to rendezvous and train at Williamsburg. Several Virginia regiments left the campus in 1776 and 1777 to join General George Washington's army in the North.

During the 1927-1931 restoration of the Sir Christopher Wren Building, portions of the foundation for Thomas Jefferson's enlargement of the building were found. The foundations were laid in 1775 but the construction on the expansion ended when the cry for independence began in the colony of Virginia. This 1930 photograph shows a portion of the foundations outside the great hall. Note the new steps in the center of the photograph. Courtesy of the Colonial Williamsburg Foundation

Peyton Randolph attended William and Mary and studied law in England. He was a member of the college's board of visitors and served as rector of the college circa 1757-1758. He also served as attorney general of the colony from 1748 to 1766. He was a member of the House of Burgesses from the college or the city of Williamsburg from 1748 to 1775, and was the first president of the Continental Congress in Philadelphia. When he died in 1776, he was buried in a crypt beneath the college chapel. This eighteenth-century portrait of Randolph is by J. Wollaston. Courtesy of the Colonial Williamsburg Foundation

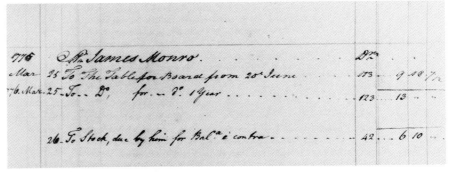

A citation from the bursar's book lists the attendance of a student, James Monro[e] at William and Mary from June 20, 1774 to March 25, 1776. According to the ledger, Monroe's fees were apparently just over twenty-two pounds for the nearly two-year stay. This is the same James Monroe who became the fifth president of the United States. Courtesy of the College Archives, College of William and Mary

James Monroe attended William and Mary between 1774 and 1776, leaving as the Revolution began to spread across the colonies. He later became the fifth president of the United States, and in 1974 his home outside Charlottesville was given to the college. This portrait of Monroe, attributed to James Herring, is in the National Portrait Gallery. Courtesy of the National Portrait Gallery, Smithsonian Institution, Washington, D.C.

THE FOUNDERS
PHI BETA KAPPA
DECEMBER 5, 1776 – JANUARY 6, 1781

JOHN HEATH

THOMAS SMITH	RICHARD BOOKER
JOHN JONES	ARMISTEAD SMITH
JOHN STUART	JOHN MOORE
DANIEL FITZHUGH	SPENCER ROANE
THEODORICK FITZHUGH	WILLIAM STITH
JOHN STORKE	WILLIAM STUART
ISAAC HITE	JOHN JAMES BECKLEY
WILLIAM SHORT	THOMAS SAVAGE
JOHN MORRISON	JOHN PAGE
GEORGE BRAXTON	WILLIAM CABELL
HENRY HILL	ELISHA PARMELE
JOHN ALLEN	GEORGE BRENT
JOHN NIVISON	PEYTON SHORT
HARTWELL COCKE	JOSEPH CABELL
THOMAS HALL	GEORGE LEE TURBERVILLE
SAMUEL HARDY	JOHN MARSHALL
ARCHIBALD STUART	BUSHROD WASHINGTON
JOHN BROWN	THOMAS LEE
PREESON BOWDOIN	LANDON CABELL
LYTTLETON EYRE	WILLIAM PIERCE
DANIEL CARROLL BRENT	RICHARD BLAND LEE
THOMAS CLEMENTS	WILLIAM MADISON
THOMAS WILLIAM BALLENDINE	JOHN SWANN
RICHARD BAKER	THOMAS COCKE

STEVENS THOMSON MASON

ALL WERE SONS OF VIRGINIA
EXCEPT ELISHA PARMELE
OF CONNECTICUT

54

Phi Beta Kappa and the Other Madison

O n Thursday, the 5th of December in the year of our Lord God one thousand seven hundred and seventy-six and the first of the Commonwealth, a happy spirit and resolution of attaining the important ends of Society entering the minds of John Heath, Thomas Smith, Richard Booker, Armistead Smith and John Jones, and afterwards seconded by others, prevailed and was accordingly ratified.

"And for the better establishment and sanctitude of our unanimity, a square silver medal was agreed on and instituted, engraved on the one side with SP, the initials of the Latin Societas Philosophiae, and on the other, agreeable to the former, with the Greek initials Φ...B...K... and an index imparting a philosophical design, extended to the three stars, a part of the planetary orb, distinguished."

Thus began the minutes of the nation's most distinguished academic society, America's first intercollegiate Greek letter fraternity, founded by students at the college. The first

This plaque in the foyer of the second Phi Beta Kappa Memorial Hall, dedicated in 1957 on the college's new campus, honors the members of Phi Beta Kappa from December 5, 1776 until January 6, 1781. On that date the last William and Mary students dispersed, many of them entering the army. The college had virtually closed by October 1780 because the armed conflict of the Revolution was advancing toward Virginia and Williamsburg. Courtesy of the Office of University Communications, College of William and Mary

meeting is believed to have been held in the Apollo Room of the historic Raleigh Tavern on Duke of Gloucester Street, just up the street from the capitol. A month later, on January 5, 1777, another session was held to adopt a mode of initiation, including an oath of fidelity. In all, twenty-five laws were established in those organizing years and the society's regulations were defined.

Four additional students were added to the rolls that day and John Heath was elected president, with Richard Booker, treasurer, and Thomas Smith, clerk. Later other students joined, including William Short on April 15, 1777. Short's membership, according to society historian Oscar M. Voorhees, proved an important event in the life of the society, serving for years as the link to the original chapter.

After continuing serious discussions, Short offered an important resolution in August 1779: "Whereas this Society is desirous that the P B K should be extended to each of the United States. Resolved, that a second Charter be granted to our Brother, Mr. Elisha Parmele, for establishing a meeting of the same in the College of New Haven [Yale] in Connecticut, to be of the same Rank, to have the same Power and to enjoy the same Priviledges with that which he is empowered to fix in the University of Cambridge [Harvard]."

It was fortuitous that the William and Mary chapter provided for an expansion of Φ B K since the Alpha Chapter ceased to function because of the impending military conflict, less than two months after the Yale chapter was organized on November 13, 1780. The third charter, to Harvard, became active September 6, 1781, nine months after William and Mary's

It was in the Apollo Room of the Raleigh Tavern that the Phi Beta Kappa Society was begun. Minutes of the society note that many other meetings were held there. After the building was reconstructed by Colonial Williamsburg in 1932, the Alpha of Virgina chapter held initiations in the room on many occasions. The Apollo Room wing of Phi Beta Kappa Memorial Hall (now Ewell Hall), dedicated in 1926, was designed to conform to the exact shape and size of the tavern room. Courtesy of the Colonial Williamsburg Foundation

"APOLLO ROOM," OLD RALEIGH TAVERN.

This old engraving of the Raleigh Tavern from Benson J. Lossing, Pictorial Field Book of the Revolution, depicts the building as it probably looked to the students of William and Mary on December 5, 1776, when five of them met in the Apollo Room and founded the Phi Beta Kappa Society, the oldest Greek-letter fraternity in America. The tavern was a meeting place of many of the great colonial patriots throughout the turbulent period of the late 1760s and 1770s. Courtesy of the Colonial Williamsburg Foundation

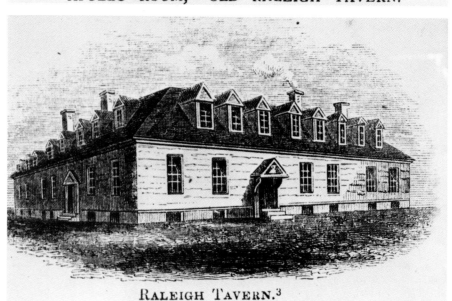

RALEIGH TAVERN.[3]

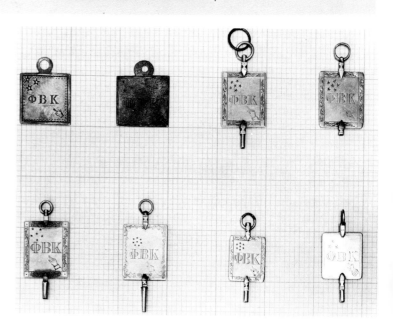

Phi Beta Kappa keys have undergone many changes in the more than 200 years since the first was struck after the founding of the society in 1776. In this collection, the Peyton Short medal at the upper left was the first; at the lower right is the one now used uniformly by all Phi Beta Kappa chapters. Harvard University's first medal is to the right of the Short medal. Courtesy of the College Archives, College of William and Mary

56

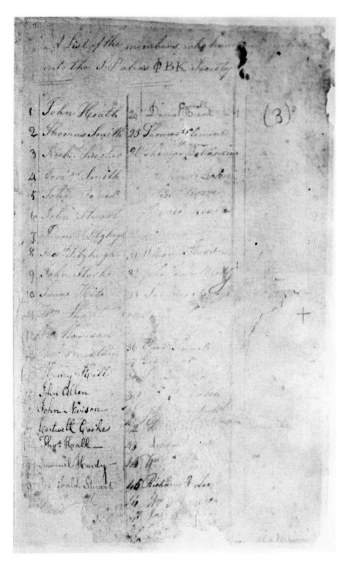

This is the membership roll, the last page, in the original minute book of the Alpha of Virginia chapter of Phi Beta Kappa at the College of William and Mary. John Heath, first president, leads the list. John Marshall, who later would become the distinguished chief justice of the United States, was the forty-first member. Courtesy of the College Archives, College of William and Mary

chapter had lapsed with the suspension of classes.

By mid-1777, the Loyalist sympathies of President Camm were causing the college serious problems in a Williamsburg climate which had fostered elements of the rebellion since 1774-1775. Camm simply could not support the new movement toward independence from England. The visitors began inquiring into the affairs of the college, including the conduct of Camm, who suddenly was removed from the presidency. He apparently attended his last faculty meeting on May 20, 1777. At the next meeting on October 23, 1777, the faculty records indicate a professor, the Reverend James Madison, had become the new president.

Madison was Virginia-born, a second cousin of the James Madison who would become the fourth president of the United States. An alumnus, he had entered the college in 1769 or 1770 and was the recipient of one of the first two Botetourt medals awarded in 1772. In May 1772, he had been appointed writing master at the school. In May 1773, he was appointed "Mathematical Professor," also while he was still "one of the Students," studying in the divinity school. He traveled to England in May 1775 for his ordination by the bishop of London, returning in the summer of 1776. He was elected minister of James City Parish in 1777; the Jamestown church was in ruins and he preached at "the Church on the Main."

Later in 1777, students of the college formed a college militia company with Madison as captain. Madison continued his professorship of natural philosophy and mathematics after being appointed president.

The visitors tried to get increased appropriations from the Virginia legislature for the school, which had seen its annual income plunge from over 5,000 pounds a few years earlier to 712 pounds in 1777. Ebenezer Hazard, surveyor general of the Post Office of the United States, visited Williamsburg in 1777 and noted that there had been no students in the divinity school for several years and "but 18 students belonging to the College, & about 30 Grammar Scholars: the College has been on the Decline for some Years." With the coming of the Revolution, the college came on leaner times.

In 1778, Jefferson offered a number of major proposals for a comprehensive educational system for the state in his bill for "The More General Diffusion of Knowledge," but the assembly did not act on them.

A major turning point in the history of

James McClurg, M.D., was a distinguished Virginia physician and an
alumnus of the college. He was
appointed the first professor of
medicine at William and Mary, with
the reorganization of 1779. He
moved to Richmond in 1785 and the
study of medicine at the college
ended. This drawing was photographed from The Stethescope, journal of the Medical Society of Virginia,
May, 1854. Courtesy of the Office of
University Communications, College
of William and Mary

George Wythe was a distinguished
lawyer in December 1779 when he
was appointed the first professor of
law and police at the college. It was
Wythe's appointment that created the
first law school in a college or university in America. Jefferson called
Wythe "the pride of the institution."
This painting is a copy by William H.
Crossman from John Trumbull's
Signers of the Declaration. Courtesy
of the Colonial Williamsburg
Foundation

One of the more historic bookplates
in a book at William and Mary. The
original bookplate of George Wythe
is found on the inside front cover of
The Twelfth Part of the Reports of Sir
Edward Coke K.T., published in 1738.
Wythe gave the book to his law pupil,
Thomas Jefferson, who willed the
volume to his friend Dabney Carr in
1806. The volume finally found its
way to the library of Tazewell Taylor
of Norfolk, who signed the book in
1842. Taylor was a William and Mary
student in 1827; he served on the
college's board of visitors in 1849
and in 1859 and as college bursar
from 1850 to 1876. Courtesy of the
Manuscript and Rare Book Department, Swem Library, College of
William and Mary

William and Mary, nevertheless, took place on December 4, 1779, when the visitors, under the leadership of Jefferson (then governor of Virginia and a board member), adopted resolutions remodeling the college and making it a university. The efforts were sincere moves designed to rekindle the college's lagging fortunes. Making changes in the structure, as the charter allowed, had become necessary; the visitors effected major reforms.

Malone, Jefferson's biographer, wrote that nothing Jefferson did or proposed in his entire career showed him more clearly to be a major American prophet than did his education plans for the state and the college. But Madison and the visitors would not support all of Jefferson's ideas; certain aspects, including a bill amending the constitution of the College of William and Mary, would have made the school a publicly-supported state university, a novel concept for its time.

Changes were necessary at William and Mary to save the school; its financial situation was worsening by the month. It was Jefferson who suggested the major curriculum changes. According to Dr. Robert Polk Thomson in his definitive work, *The Reform of the College of William and Mary, 1762-1780*, the Brafferton master had to stay under the terms of its endowment, but the other five professorships were altered employing the exact phraseology Jefferson used in his earlier bill. They became professorships of law and police; anatomy and medicine; natural philosophy and mathematics; moral philosophy, the law of nature and of nations and the fine arts; and modern languages. The grammar school and the two professorships of divinity and oriental languages were abolished and the study of law, medicine, and the fine arts instituted, the first such studies in any American college. Jefferson's proposals for a chair of history and a chair of ancient languages were not approved.

The reform, later dubbed the "Jeffersonian Reorganization," went further. Jefferson would have placed ordinary government of the college in the hands of the faculty, but the new statute added a committee from the visitors to meet with the president and masters and determine what would be taught in each field. It was an action which greatly curtailed the professors' freedom in the area of instruction, but the faculty accepted it without comment. The visitors also dropped the professors' fixed salaries. Each student would pay 1,000 pounds of tobacco to each professor under whom he studied.

On December 29, 1779, the new faculty endorsed the reforms. Madison continued as president and professor of natural philosophy and mathematics; Robert Andrews, professor of moral philosophy since 1777, had the expanded title of professor of moral philosophy, the law of nature and nations, and the fine arts; Charles Bellini assumed the modern languages chair; George Wythe was professor of law and police; James McClurg was professor of anatomy and medicine and the Brafferton post remained unfilled. The grammar school was abolished and John Bracken, therefore, lost his faculty status and eventually brought suit against the college.

The faculty adopted new school terms to run from October until April and from May to August. The first elective system of studies was introduced with students selecting as many or as few sets of lectures as they wanted for a given term and in any order they determined. An honor system, the first in the nation, was established. The old end of the term declamations were retained.

"The plan for the college was unlike any other in England or America. Breathtaking in its simplicity, the reformed curriculum was a hybrid incorporating the old and the new, the pragmatic and the visionary," Dr. Thomson wrote. The oath to the king was repudiated, but the college did not break its ties with the Anglican Church; they were merely lessened. There also was no longer a chancellor in London, but the college never abandoned the royal charter during reorganization nor during the Revolution that followed.

In the late winter of 1779, taking a break from the war and availing himself of the new changes in rules, John Marshall enrolled at William and Mary,

This silhouette of Robert Andrews is the only known depiction of the colonial professor. Andrews joined the college faculty in 1777, and in 1779 when the college became a university, he became professor of moral philosophy, the law of nature and of nations and the fine arts. He was the first college or university professor in America to include the fine arts as a part of his curriculum. Andrews later became professor of mathematics and was the bursar of the college until his death in 1805. Courtesy of the College Archives, College of William and Mary

probably more motivated to be near his beloved Polly Ambler in Yorktown than to gain an education. According to Leonard Baker in his biography, *John Marshall, A Life in Law,* Marshall, who would later become chief justice of the United States, stayed at the college only for two or three months, but "enough time to make some valuable acquaintances," including classmate Bushrod Washington (a nephew of George Washington) and Professor Wythe.

Marshall's primary college interest was in Wythe's law lectures, and the notes from his classes survive, covering nearly 200 manuscript pages. Marshall apparently was a popular and earnest student, Baker wrote, and on May 18, 1780, Marshall was inducted into the Phi Beta Kappa fraternity. Marshall was assigned a debate topic to prepare for a meeting of ΦBK, "Whether any form of government is more favourable to public virtue than a Commonwealth?"—but there is no record of Marshall's argument.

According to Madison in a letter dated August 1, 1780, to President Ezra Stiles of Yale, the reorganization was successful and stimulated student interest: "The number of Students is more considerable than heretofore and encreases daily." Jefferson echoed those words, writing to James Madison, Jr., in the congress in Philadelphia: "Our new Institution at the College has had a success which has gained it universal applause." He noted the popularity of Wythe's courses.

Unfortunately, the euphoria was short-lived. By October 27, 1780, according to one student, the college was "intirely deserted by every Student but one or two who are sick;" President Madison was "talking of resigning his Professorship, & the Students all turned Soldiers & everything in the utmost Confusion."

Also in 1780, the capital of Virginia moved from Williamsburg inland to Richmond because of the war. Movement of the state's politial center cut the nerve of the old royal college. The political and social support, which could have helped sustain William and Mary in later years, would not be forthcoming. The days of William and Mary being called a school of statesmen were numbered. Hard times would plague the school for at least the next 140 years.

By January 1781, Madison wrote: "The University is a Desart. We were in a very flourishing way before the first invasion...but we are now entirely dispersed." Classes did not resume until the fall of 1782. Charles, Lord Cornwallis, the

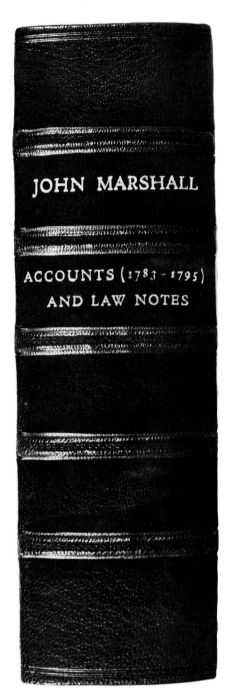

JOHN MARSHALL

ACCOUNTS (1783 - 1795)
AND LAW NOTES

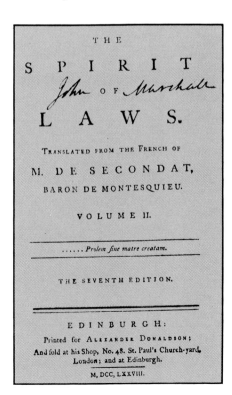

THE

SPIRIT *John* OF *Marshall* LAWS.

TRANSLATED FROM THE FRENCH OF

M. DE SECONDAT,

BARON DE MONTESQUIEU.

VOLUME II.

...... *Prolem fine matre creatam.*

THE SEVENTH EDITION.

EDINBURGH:
Printed for ALEXANDER DONALDSON;
And fold at his Shop, No. 48. St. Paul's Church-yard,
London; and at Edinburgh.

M, DCC, LXXVIII.

The law notes which John Marshall took during his classes with George Wythe survive and have provided an interesting look into the academic study of law in 1780. The notes were utilized in a study of Marshall's law background and were reprinted in the first volume of the multivolume historical work, The Papers of John Marshall, *currently being published by the Institute of Early American History and Culture and the College of William and Mary. Courtesy of the College Archives, College of William and Mary*

John Marshall was a student at William and Mary for two or three months in the spring of 1780, while he was taking a break from the Revolution. While at the college, his primary interest was in the law classes of Professor George Wythe. On May 18, 1780, Marshall was inducted into the Phi Beta Kappa Society. Courtesy of the Manuscript and Rare Book Department, Swem Library, College of William and Mary

The Earl Gregg Swem Library at William and Mary has an extensive collection of books associated with John Marshall as well as a collection of manuscripts. Courtesy of the Manuscript and Rare Book Department, Swem Library, College of William and Mary

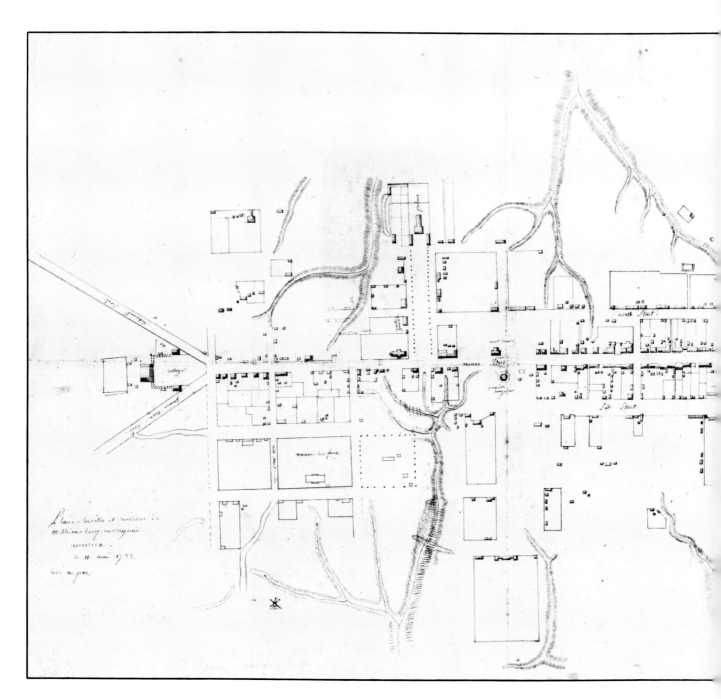

This is the "Temple seal," the second seal of the College of William and Mary. Following the Revolution, the old seal, perhaps considered too much a reminder of royal rule, ceased to be used. The Temple seal was first used by the college in 1783. This photograph is of a twentieth-century wax impression. Courtesy of the Manuscript and Rare Book Department, Swem Library, College of William and Mary; Henry Grunder photo

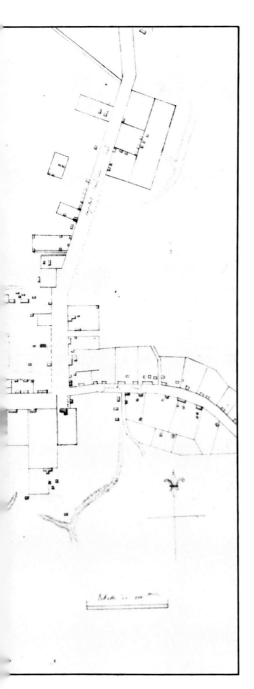

In 1781 or 1782, while the French army was in the vicinity of Williamsburg, a French cartographer drew this map of the area. The Frenchman's Map of Williamsburg is the most detailed account of the structures in the area. Note the college at the far left at the end of the Duke of Gloucester Street, which runs almost the entire length of the map; the courthouse and green in the middle, and the capitol building and its green at the right. There are numerous outbuildings associated with the college and an area in the rear that apparently was "college camp," where soldiers had camped periodically since 1776. Courtesy of the Manuscript and Rare Book Department, Swem Library, College of William and Mary

THE COMMONWEALTH OF VIRGINIA to *George Rogers Clark*, Gentleman, greeting: KNOW YOU that our Governour being duly certified of your Ability and good Character, hath constituted you the said *George Rogers Clark* Surveyor of the, with Authority to execute the said Office, and to take for so doing the Fees allowed by Law: SAVING AND RESERVING to the President and Professors of the College of *William* & *Mary* one sixth part of the legal Fees which shall be received by you. IN TESTIMONY whereof these our Letters are made patent. WITNESS ~~Thomas Jefferson~~ *Benjamin Harrison*, Esquire, our said Governour at *Richmond* the *Ninth* Day of *February* in the Year of our Lord One Thousand Seven Hundred and *eighty four*

Benj Harrison

The Fees due to the College was paid by William Croghan who took up this from the College

After Virginia became a state, William and Mary retained the right to issue surveyor's licenses. This license of George Rogers Clark was issued in Richmond on February 9, 1784, and was signed by Governor Benjamin Harrison. Clark later explored the great Louisiana Territory with Meriweather Lewis for President Thomas Jefferson. Courtesy of the College Archives, College of William and Mary

St. George Tucker was the second
professor of law and police at
William and Mary from 1791 to
1804. His Commentaries on Blackstone became the first American law
textbook. Courtesy of the College
Archives, College of William
and Mary

St. George Tucker signed the title
page of this book, which apparently
was given to him by Thomas Jefferson. Courtesy of the Tucker-Coleman
Papers, Manuscript and Rare Book
Department, Swem Library, College
of William and Mary

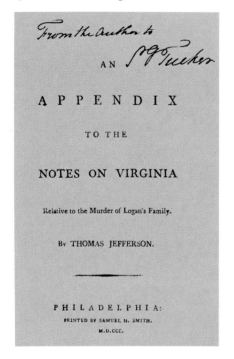

In March 1790, an honorary degree
was given by the faculty of William
and Mary to St. George Tucker, who
would succeed George Wythe as the
professor of law and police in 1791.
Tucker was considered an outstanding scholar and one of the leading
lawyers of his time. Signing the
diploma were James Madison, college
president; Robert Andrews, mathematics professor; and Charles Bellini,
professor of modern languages. Courtesy of the Tucker-Coleman Papers,
canuscript and Rare Book Department, Swem Library, College of
William and Mary

British commander, made the President's house his Williamsburg headquarters for some days in June 1781, prior to the climactic Battle of Yorktown. During the battle and after the surrender, the college's main building was used as a French army hospital, and in November 1781 the President's House, occupied by wounded French officers, was severely damaged by a fire which destroyed all Madison's books. Madison, who had left Williamsburg, returned in February or early March 1782, and was forced to live in town, in what is now called the Archibald Blair House, until the President's House could be repaired at the expense of the French King Louis XVI and his army. The work was completed in 1786.

Madison and his small faculty were rich in energy and scholarship. Wythe, who had attended the college briefly, was a top-ranked classical scholar and lawyer, whom Jefferson called "the pride of the institution," and "one of the greatest men of the age, always distinguished by the most spotless virtue." After the college reopened in October 1782, Wythe returned as professor of law and police until 1789 when he became chancellor of Virginia and moved to Richmond. Wythe was succeeded by St. George Tucker, a judge of the general court, whose *Commentaries of Blackstone* became the first American textbook on the law.

James McClurg, professor of anatomy and medicine, had been a student of the college and had completed his medical education at the University of Edinburgh and on the continent. His medical reputation was well-known, and during the Revolution he served as physician general and director of hospitals for the Virginia troops. Unfortunately, nothing is known about his course offering.

Robert Andrews, a graduate of the College of Philadelphia, studied drawing while in school, and apparently through his inclusion of fine arts in his professorship in 1779, began to implement Jefferson's concept of the fine arts. Andrews succeeded Madison as mathematics professor in 1784 and Madison added moral philosophy to his natural philosophy lectures. Andrews also served until 1804 as bursar of the college, handling all its finances.

Charles Bellini, professor of modern languages, had been recommended by Jefferson and taught French, Italian, Spanish, and German. Madison was also considered a fine lecturer and was the first person to introduce into a college a regular system of lectures on political economy. When his health was good, Madison was known to have lectured from four to six hours a day.

By 1784 there were about eighty students, and Madison, having lost all of his own books and papers in the President's House fire of 1781, realized that the students required more books for studies. He attempted to build up a library of "ancient authors." Books were obtained as gifts from friends in England, and at the request of the marquis de Chastellux, King Louix XVI sent "200 books in beautiful editions," from France. The general assembly turned over certain state lands near Williamsburg to the president and professors at William and Mary to be disposed of in the best "interest and advantage of the said university."

Unfortunately, Dr. McClurg moved to Richmond in about 1785 and the study of medicine ended. Later that year, Madison's cousin James, who would become the fourth president of the United States, received an honorary doctor of laws degree in absentia. On April 30, 1788, George Washington, in a letter to Samuel Griffin, rector of the college, accepted office as the first American chancellor of William and Mary. Washington served throughout his presidency and until his death in 1799; thus his first and last public offices came from William and Mary.

George Washington served his last public office as chancellor of William and Mary, beginning in 1788 before he became the first president of the United States and ending in 1799 when he died. Courtesy of the Office of University Communications, College of William and Mary

THE
RIGHT HONOURABLE
NORBORNE BERKELEY
BARON DE BOTETOURT
HIS MAJESTY'S
LATE LIEUTENANT AND
GOVERNOR GENERAL OF THE
COLONY AND DOMINION
OF VIRGINIA

Chapter Seven
1790-1849

A Struggle to Survive

The reorganization of William and Mary effected in 1779 by the visitors and endorsed by the faculty still was an irritant for the governing board in 1790, when the dismissal of John Bracken, the master of the grammar school, finally wound its way through court. The college's counsel was attorney John Marshall, who had attended classes briefly at William and Mary in 1780 and was admitted to the bar following the Revolution.

Bracken had lost his faculty rank when the reorganization took place. His case, begun in 1787, finally reached the Virginia Court of Appeals, where Marshall contended that William and Mary was a private, rather than a public institution, and therefore subject only to the terms set forth by the founder (the crown) in the royal charter, and secondly, that in any case, the visitors had acted within their authority as defined in the charter.

Another alumnus, John Taylor, argued for Bracken, contending that after the revolution and independence, the commonwealth of Vir-

The statue of Lord Botetourt was purchased by the college faculty about 1801 and moved from the capitol building where it stood for many years in the yard in front of the Sir Christopher Wren Building. Courtesy of the Office of University Communications, College of William and Mary

ginia was the only true heir to the rights and privileges of the crown. Therefore, only the state, not the visitors, could amend the constitution of the college.

Marshall's position prevailed, but later, when Bracken became the college president, the case he pressed so diligently would cause him trouble within the college family. (Later, in the famous Dartmouth College case argued before the United States Supreme Court, Chief Justice Marshall repeated his same arguments in giving his famous opinion that a charter is a contract between the grantees and the grantor and the contract cannot later be altered, without consent of the ensuing grantees and the grantor.)

Madison continued to maintain a strong faculty, and in 1788 Jefferson wrote a friend that Williamsburg was "a remarkably healthy situation, reasonably cheap, and affords very genteel society. I know no place in the world, while the present professors remain, where I would as soon place a son." However, by 1804, of the old guard of professors—Madison, Andrews, Wythe, Bellini, and McClurg—only Madison remained. But other good professors took their place.

Samuel Miller in *A Retrospect of the Eighteenth Century,* published in New York in 1803, listed all the college's professorships and the books used by each professor. He added, "There is probably no College in the United States in which political science is studied with so much ardour, and in which it is considered so pre-eminently a favourite object, as in this."

The professors and students secured a statue that would become a symbol of William

Diploma

This diploma of David Yancy, written in Latin, is the oldest known surviving William and Mary student diploma. It was awarded in 1795 by the "University of William and Mary," and is signed by the college president, James Madison, and the other professors. Courtesy of the College Archives, College of William and Mary

This unusual silhouette, of the Reverend James Madison, William and Mary president from 1777 to 1812, is from a rare and early collection in the Library of Congress. It is a copy by Mariette Minningerode Andrews made from an original, cut during his lifetime. Courtesy of the College Archives, College of William and Mary

and Mary in the nineteenth and twentieth centuries, the marble statue of Lord Botetourt, originally placed on the capitol piazza in 1773. It was defaced between 1780 and 1790, during the anti-English sentiment. In 1801 the statue was purchased by the faculty from the state for $100 and moved to the college yard. One of the oldest examples of colonial American statuary, it represented for the college a man who had loved and supported William and Mary, and who was considered "the best of governors and the best of men."

Accounts of student riots in 1802 and 1808 apparently were greatly exaggerated and reports of college property destroyed were without basis, although riots were reported in certain northern newspapers. Madison died at the President's House on March 6, 1812, and people believed the college would fail without him. William Nelson, judge of the general court and the college law professor, wrote of Madison: "The support he lent to this ancient seminary of learning is now at an end, and there is cause of serious apprehension that the fabric itself will fall a victim to premature delapidation."

When the Reverend John Bracken was selected to succeed Madison, there were only forty-four students enrolled. Bracken had returned to the college in 1792, when two professorships of humanity were established. He served as professor of humanity in the reestablished grammar school from the time of his return until 1812. His selection as president, which occurred immediately after Madison's funeral service, caused more than one visitor to be surprised by the "rude shock" of the appointment.

According to Ruby O. Osborne in her detailed manuscript, *The College of William and Mary in Virginia, 1800-1827*, Bracken was sixty-seven when he became president. He had received a doctor of divinity degree from the college in 1793, and a few months after becoming president was elected the bishop of the Protestant Episcopal Church in Virginia, also succeeding Madison. He was never ordained bishop and resigned his church post a year later.

In July 1812, the college advertised to fill two faculty vacancies and apparently classes continued despite a lack of professors. The grammar school had been closed again. In June 1813, faculty records indicate that examinations were interrupted by "the Occupancy of the College as Barracks for the Militia," since war with Great Britain

In 1795 a "premium" was given to the student who gave the best oratory. This medal was awarded to John Mumford Walker. Courtesy of the College Archives, College of William and Mary

had been declared a year earlier. On one occasion, the militia, thinking English soldiers had entered the town, "made such haste to get out, that men, officers, and all, not able to see their way in the dark, stumbled and rolled down the long flight of stairs leading to the ground floor."

Since 1795, the visitors had been noted for their absence. Madison wrote in 1800, in an effort to abolish the grammar school (reestablished in 1792 with Bracken as headmaster), that the visitors had not met in five years, and subsequent records indicate they met infrequently, mostly during emergencies. Bracken displayed little leadership and the grudges held over from the time of his lawsuit, twenty years earlier, had not abated. Jefferson, in a letter to his friend William Short in November 1813, called Bracken a "simpleton."

In the spring of 1814, the visitors resolved "that the Right Revd John Bracken...be requested to inform this Convocation in direct and explicit Terms whether or not he will consent to resign his office...." Bracken was the last college president born in England.

By August 29, 1814, Dr. John Augustine Smith had been elected president, the first layman to hold the post. (The visitors repealed the statute that called for a member of the clergy to be president.) When elected, Smith, an 1800 graduate of William and Mary, was serving as professor of anatomy, surgery, and physiology at Columbia

College in New York.

Upon his arrival, Smith reported "not a single Lecture-Room properly fitted up...& the whole establishment...tending rapidly to ruin," primarily due to leaks in the roof. Rooms, however, were repaired and efforts made to attract more students.

Smith made it a practice at the first of his tenure to begin each session with a series of lectures. In 1816 the topic was politics, and when the lectures were published in book form in 1817, *A Syllabus of the Lectures Delivered to the Senior Students in the College of William and Mary on Government* became one of the first United States textbooks on American government. Attendance at the school increased in Smith's first years, with an enrollment of ninety-five students in the fall of 1816, possibly the highest enrollment thus far in the school's history.

By 1816 a movement began in Albemarle County to establish a college in the area, Central College. The proposal was approved by the general assembly, a major step in the ultimate development of a Jefferson-designed state university. According to Osborne, William and Mary was no longer an institution at the apex of its education pyramid. Jefferson periodically wrote at this time about "the long and lingering decline of William and Mary."

The assembly continued discussions, through its committees, about the establishment of a "University of Virginia." Many William and Mary visitors

This painting of the college building is believed to have been completed about 1820. Note the porch above and the columns on either side of the main doorway. The statue of Lord Botetourt was placed in front of the building in 1801. Courtesy of the Office of University Communications, College of William and Mary

were convinced that the college would naturally be that university, even going so far as to approve two new members from Albemarle County and two from Richmond, well outside the traditional forty-mile radius from campus, long considered best for board members.

Jefferson, of course, had other plans, and with Cabell worked diligently to have the university placed at Central College. Such external forces worked to the detriment of the growth and prosperity of the College of William and Mary. Jefferson, in fact, wrote in 1818 to Francis Gilmer: "I trust you did not for a moment seriously think of shutting yourself behind the door of William and Mary College. A more complete *cul de sac* could

not be proposed to you." Enrollment, as would be expected, declined during this time, with only fifty students attending in the fall of 1818, a drop of forty-two students.

On January 25, 1819, the legislature resolved that the proposed Central College, still a school on paper only, would become "The University of Virginia." Of the first seven university visitors, all but one were William and Mary alumni.

Believing that a "more liberal plan with respect to the conferring of degrees" would be beneficial to William and Mary, the faculty voted on March 30, 1821 "that the Degree of Bachelor of Arts...be bestowed on Students of two Years' Standing, and the degree of Master of Arts upon

John Augustine Smith was president of William and Mary from 1814 to 1826; he was the first layman to hold the post. Courtesy of the College Art Collection, College of William and Mary

those of three Years' Standing."

In the fall of 1824, the marquis de Lafayette announced his intention to visit Williamsburg, and the college and the faculty decided to hold a reception where the president would make a suitable address and the college would confer on the general the honorary doctor of laws degree.

Enrollment at William and Mary was down to only thirty-five students by 1824 and Smith told the visitors on July 5, 1824, at their annual meeting, "The University of Virginia, which is just about to go into operation, can not but affect us." The president added that he was "quite satisfied that there is but one possible expedient, & that is a transfer of the establishment to Richmond." All but one of the professors supported the move.

The board appointed a committee to consider Smith's proposal, and, through several committees, the Virginia General Assembly even considered the transfer of the college to Richmond. Land in Richmond was offered to the college for a campus, gifts of money were used as enticements, and it was even suggested that a medical school could be instituted. On November 26, 1824, the visitors also endorsed the proposed move by a narrow 8-6 vote. About a week later, however, citizens of Williamsburg assembled at the courthouse to protest the possible removal to the legislature, charging that the visitors did not have the power to approve the move without violating the college's charter.

When the general assembly took up the removal issue in January-February 1825, John Tyler led the opposition, making a major speech in the legislature. Tyler's effort, along with a Jefferson scheme—to dissolve William and Mary, divide the state into ten college districts, and establish ten new schools throughout Virginia with William and Mary's money—caused many concerns for legislators who supported the move. In light of the alternative—Jefferson's Bill—college friends began to withdraw support for the removal bill, which was ultimately defeated.

On October 12, 1825, John Page wrote from Williamsburg to St. George Tucker, then in Nelson County, comparing William and Mary and the newly established University of Virginia: "I am clearly of the opinion if the public were well informed of the actual condition of each [class], and disposed to patronise Literature equally where ever it was to be found in the State William and Mary would have nothing to fear from the University."

In July 1826, there were forty students in the grammar school, but only twenty-one students, including two graduate students, attending college courses. Smith, who had supported the move of the college to Richmond, then decided to accept an offer and rejoin the faculty of the College of Physicians and Surgeons in New York, becoming the school's president in 1831.

In December 1826, Dr. William Holland Wilmer arrived as the new William and Mary president, coming to Williamsburg from St. Paul's Church in Alexandria, where he had established, with the Reverend William Meade, the Virginia Theological Seminary. He had supported the theological professorship at William and Mary, which was established in 1821 and which ended with the opening of the Alexandria seminary in 1823.

During Wilmer's brief one-year term, he was instructed to ascertain "what Repairs are requisite

John Tyler, president of the United States from 1841 to 1845, an alumnus of William and Mary, was on the board of visitors from about 1825 until his death in 1862. Tyler opposed moving the college from Williamsburg to Richmond, and made impassioned appeals before the Virginia General Assembly in 1824 and 1825. He later served as rector of the college from 1840 to 1842, while he was president, and again from 1848 to 1862. He was named chancellor of the college in 1859, and his son Lyon G. Tyler served as William and Mary president from 1888 to 1919. Courtesy of the National Portrait Gallery, Smithsonian Institution, Washington, D.C.

William Barton Rogers was a professor at William and Mary from 1828 to 1835. An alumnus of the college, he later founded the Massachusetts Institute of Technology. This portrait is by Bethuel Moore and was a gift of college president John Stewart Bryan in 1938. Courtesy of the College Art Collection, College of William and Mary

in College and about the premises" and to secure appropriate estimates. Unfortunately, he died at the President's House on July 24, 1827, before all the work could be accomplished, but a report to the visitors from Wilmer earlier in the month showed eighty students in college, an increase of thirty-nine students in one year. Wilmer, who also had served as rector of Bruton Parish Church, was buried in the chancel of the church.

The Reverend Adam Empie was elected president and arrived in Williamsburg in December 1827, after the school term began. A graduate of Union College, Empie had entered the ministry and served at several Episcopal parishes in New York and North Carolina before coming to the college. Early in his administration the college had a full complement of professors, including Empie, also professor of rhetoric and *belles lettres*; Judge James Semple, professor of law and police; Dr. Thomas Roderick Dew, professor of history and political law; Ferdinand Campbell Stewart, professor of mathematics, Charles de la Pena, professor of modern languages; and Dr. William Barton Rogers, professor of chemistry and natural philosophy. Rogers, a William and Mary graduate, later moved to Boston and in 1865 founded the Massachusetts Institute of Technology.

Like Smith before him, Empie continued the practice of The Brafferton being run by a steward, who boarded and lodged college students, the Indian school having ended just prior to the Revolution. Morning prayers for students and faculty were held daily in the chapel.

Students during Empie's tenure seemed to misbehave as much as at other times in the school's history. Some students destroyed college property, including a few records, while others harassed the professors; in 1832 students paraded a horse "through the upper passages of the college" building, and in 1835, forced "a poor old horse" up the stairs into another student's bedroom.

Attendance ranged from a high of about 113 in 1829 to a low of fifty-eight in 1834 when the law course was discontinued for lack of a professor. During Empie's presidency he was allowed "to keep his cows in the back yard of the College," which may have inspired, a few years later, the now famous sketch depicting cows on the campus, drawn by Thomas Millington, son of a college professor; it is dated about 1840. A tornado struck the college in June 1834, and damage was considerable.

Empie's nine years were relatively uneventful;

The Reverend Adam Empie served as president of William and Mary from 1827 to 1836. His portrait, along with those of a number of his predecessors and successors, hangs in the presidents' gallery on the second floor of the Sir Christopher Wren Building. Courtesy of the College Art Collection, College of William and Mary

This is a wash drawing of the main building, The Brafferton (left), and the President's House (right) by Thomas Millington, son of William and Mary professor John Millington. He is believed to have drawn it about 1838-1840, and it is probably the basis for his famous lithograph, circa 1840. Courtesy of the College Archives, College of William and Mary

WILLIAM AND MARY COLLEGE, WILLIAMSBURG, VA.

This is one of several versions of the Thomas Millington lithograph, circa 1840, showing the cows on the campus. It is not believed to be the original. Courtesy of the College Archives, College of William and Mary

This painting, also by Thomas Millington, shows a portion of Duke of Gloucester Street with the college building in the middle and Bruton Parish Church at right. Courtesy of the College Archives, College of William and Mary

Order
OF THE
COLLEGIATE EXERCISES
ON THE
4th of July.

INTRODUCTORY PRAYER.

ORATIONS.

1. EULOGY ON *Thomas Jefferson*—by Thos. Martin.
2. ORATION ON *Ancient and Modern Literature*—by C. Q. Tompkins.
3. " On *Modern improvements in Natural Philosophy*—by George W. Semple.
*4. " On *the History and Advantages of Commerce*—by Edmund P. Oliver.
*5. " On *the Influence of our Retrospective Emotions upon our present condition and future views*—by Jno. D. Munford.
*6. " On *the Profession of the Law*—by Jas. N. McPherson.
7. " On *the Art of Printing and the Advantages of a Free Press*—by Ro. Ridley.
8. " On *the influence of Luxury upon the Social and Political condition of Man*—by Wm. W. Wingfield.
9. " On *Honour*—by Alfred Johns.
*10. " On *American Jurisprudence*—by Edward Simmons.
11. " On *the True Glory of a Nation*—by James B. Watts.
12. " On *the Influence of the Arts and Sciences upon the Moral and Political Condition of Mankind*—by Cyrus A. Griffin.
13. " On *the comparative merits of the Warrior and Philosopher*—by Edward I. Young.
14. " On *the Progress of Civilization and the Present Prospects of the World*—by Geo. B'ow.
15. " On *the Day*—by Thomas H. Daniel.

Degrees delivered to the Candidates by the President.

Baccalaureate Address.

CONCLUDING PRAYER.

N. B.—The Asterisk designates those who are absent from town, and those who, though present, have been prevented, by indisposition, from preparing for the public exercises.

Graduation exercises on July 4, 1831, were a lengthy occasion. On this date there was a eulogy on Thomas Jefferson and fourteen orations by the graduating students. In addition, there was a baccalaureate address. Courtesy of the College Archives, College of William and Mary

Thomas Roderick Dew was college president from 1836 to 1846. Dew brought a revival to William and Mary. Considered a superb teacher, Dew always tried to hire the best faculty available. "To him to be a professor was to be one who speaks out from the depths of his own being, and not the utterer of polished platitudes," a later college president wrote of Dew. Courtesy of the College Art Collection, College of William and Mary

they were free of turmoil and division, unlike during Smith's term. Empie resigned in 1836 to become minister of the St. James' Church in Richmond and Thomas Roderick Dew, a William and Mary alumnus and faculty member, succeeded to the presidency.

College enrollment jumped significantly, from 66 students in 1835 to a record high of about 140 students in 1839. This increase occurred, ironically, during a period of economic recession. Students seem to have been less destructive of college property than were some earlier students, but by 1844 student enrollment was down to 69. Dew encouraged a variety of activities at the college, including the founding, on July 4, 1842, of the Society of the Alumni; he became the organization's first president.

Dew continued to maintain a strong faculty, including Judge Nathaniel Beverly Tucker, professor of law and police; Dr. John Millington, professor of chemistry and natural philosophy; Robert Saunders, professor of mathematics; and Charles Minnigerode, professor of humanity, the German who introduced Williamsburg residents to their first Christmas tree in 1843.

Unfortunately, a number of the "venerable old elm trees of a noble growth" around the college died in 1843. According to Professor Tucker, an insect attacked the Dutch elms: "The bug itself attacks and injures the leaves. The worm then appears...about the first of July, and in ten days the trees are stripped." By 1845 new trees had been planted at the college, protected by "Tin work and Lead rings." Thirteen years later $500 was given by General John Cocke to "replace the old Elms in the college yard, with native Elms."

Dew's various accomplishments at the college have been detailed by a later president, John Stewart Bryan. Dew was considered a superb teacher and he attempted always to hire the best professors. "When we consider the revival he wrought in the strength of William and Mary, the influence he exerted on dominant political issues in the South, and the impression he left upon students under his guidance, we see that he was correct in the valuation that he placed upon a position at William and Mary." Bryan wrote, "To him to be a professor was to be one who speaks out from the depths of his own being, and not the utterer of polished platitudes. As he saw it, the province of the professor is not solely to comment oracularly on what happened in the past, but knowing the past in its fulness, to proclaim

prophetically how man can control the future."

During these years, a host of later nineteenth-century personages were students at the college, including generals, doctors, lawyers, and historians. The roll call of representative Virginia families was impressive, including General Winfield Scott; John J. Crittenden, later governor of Kentucky and United States attorney general; James Beale, noted physician; General William B. Taliaferro; D.C. Dejarnette and Charles L. Scott, later congressmen; Richard Coke, later governor of Texas; and numerous students with the surnames of Page, Cabell, Harrison, Nelson and Byrd, families long tied to Virginia history.

Dr. Herbert B. Adams, associate professor of history at Johns Hopkins University, in his pamphlet, *The College of William and Mary: A Contribution to the History of Higher Education, with Suggestions for its National Promotion,* wrote in 1887 that in addition to the colonial statesmen who attended the college—Benjamin Harrison, Thomas Jefferson, Carter Braxton, Thomas Nelson, and George Wythe, signers of the Declaration of Independence; Peyton Randolph, Edmund Randolph, John Blair, James Innes, John Marshall, and three presidents of the United States—there were also twenty members of Congress, thirty-seven judges, fifteen U.S. Senators, seventeen governors and numerous army and navy officers.

Regarding the college's nineteenth-century impact, Dr. Adams wrote, "If any justification were to be sought for the national idea in education, it might be found in the historical influence of a single institution like the College of William and Mary upon the entire South. . . .[it] sent currents of intellectual life throughout every southern state."

Dew raised the college "to as great prosperity as perhaps had ever been its lot at any time since its first establishment," wrote Virginia Episcopal Bishop Meade. Unfortunately, Dew died in Paris, August 6, 1846, on his wedding trip.

No minutes from the board of visitors of this period survive, but *A Digest of the Proceedings of the Conventions and Councils in the Diocese of Virginia,* published in 1883, adds a little-known aspect of college history. Records of the convention of May 1847 indicate that the diocese assistant bishop, John Johns, was "elected President of William and Mary College and Professor of the Moral Chair with great unanimity" by the board of visitors on February 24, 1847. The visitors talked with Johns about becoming president, but he had not accepted. At the convention, the diocese voted to advise Johns not to take the post and he declined it.

Robert Saunders, Jr., professor of mathematics, was named president pro tem, while the board courted Johns, and on October 12, 1847, Saunders was formally elected president. His two years as college president were a period of contention between faculty and the board of visitors, with the question of a university in Richmond being raised again. Some faculty members supported the move, but townspeople strongly objected, with similar concerns as when the Richmond move was debated earlier, in 1824-25. Professor John Millington wrote to Professor Joseph Henry of the Smithsonian Institution on May 30, 1848, that since the death of President Dew "acts of Nepotism have disturbed our former peace—a schism exists between the Faculty & the Visitors and as a means of checking this, the Visitors have requested the whole faculty to resign which request has been complied with."

Saunders resigned with the other faculty members. The visitors had been deliberating the appointment of Benjamin Stoddert Ewell as professor of mathematics. He had served from 1839 to 1846 as professor of mathematics and natural philosophy at Hampden-Sydney College and was appointed in 1846 as professor of mathematics and military science at Washington College (now Washington and Lee University). With the faculty resignation and the departure of Saunders, the board offered Ewell the presidency. In a letter to Robert McCandlish, dated August 3, 1848, Ewell wrote, "As I cannot flatter myself that the board of visitors of William and Mary College could have elected me to the presidency had my meager qualifications been fully known, I feel compelled to decline. In case it should be deemed expedient I would not object to filling the presidency till such time as the visitors shall see fit to make another choice."

While agreeing to serve as acting president, Ewell also accepted the post as professor of mathematics. During Ewell's stewardship only classes in law and the grammar school were continued during the 1848-1849 school term. Following Ewell's letter, the visitors immediately renewed their efforts to get Johns to accept the presidency, and two months later, in October 1848, Johns was again elected William and Mary president. This time the offer was approved by the church convention in May 1849, provided Johns could occupy the President's House, have little salary, bring Dr. Silas Totten to the faculty as professor of moral philosophy, and continue with some of his duties as assistant bishop of the diocese.

Although Ewell signed documents and faculty minutes as William and Mary president and ordered and directed substantial repairs to the college buildings during 1848-1849, it is evident from his correspondence that he declined the permanent job and his presidency was merely as an acting, pro-tem situation. This is further supported by the fact that the visitors formally elected Johns as president just a few weeks after Ewell came to campus, even though Johns did not take office until July 1849. Thus, Ewell, with his one-year presidency, 1848-1849, probably should not be counted among the college's full term presidents; other acting presidents have not been counted and the numbering system of the presidents may be off by one. The new William and Mary president, expected to take office in 1985, will be the twenty-fourth, instead of the twenty-fifth president.

Robert Saunders, Jr., became professor of mathematics in 1833 and continued his professorship when he was named acting president of William and Mary in 1846; within a year he was named full president, but this tenure ended in 1848 when friction between the faculty and the board of visitors arose and his entire faculty was forced out. This portrait is by George Bagby Matthews. Courtesy of the College Art Collection, College of William and Mary

Chapter Eight
1849-1888

Ravages of War and "The Old Bell Ringer"

T he selection of Bishop John Johns as president represented a major effort of the visitors to reorganize the school and nurture the now-tenuous ties with the Episcopal Church. After a year's suspension of college classes, Johns began serving William and Mary in 1849, while still carrying his title and responsibilities as assistant bishop. Johns had insisted that Dr. Silas Totten take on the duties of professor of moral philosophy to be paid from his salary. Involved also in administrative duties at the college, Totten was a former president of Trinity College in Hartford, Connecticut.

Recognized by his fellow Episcopalians as the greatest preacher of his day, Johns was able to reassemble a competent faculty and fill all the available positions, including law, chemistry and natural philosophy, mathematics, ancient languages, rhetoric and moral philosophy, and philosophy and political economy. Enrollment also increased from twenty-one students in 1849 to eighty-three students in

The Right Reverend John Johns was the associate bishop of the diocese of Virginia and became president of William and Mary in 1849. The board of visitors initially had asked Johns to accept the presidency in 1846, but the diocese convention of May 1847 rejected the proposal. Johns resigned as president in 1854 and later became bishop of the diocese. The portrait is by J. R. Lambdin and was painted in 1856. Courtesy of the College Art Collection, College of William and Mary

1853-1854, with eleven of the students studying law.

In his personal journal Totten recorded the events of his ten years at William and Mary. Arriving in October 1849, he observed that in Williamsburg "the trees, the grass, the houses, were all begrimed with dust." He had no better view of the college: "Such a miserable unsightly pile of bricks, such dirty passages and strange inconvenient rooms and broken walls within I had never seen before. It did not seem possible that such a college could prosper or that respectable young men would be content to live in such a building. If I had hopes for a large income from the money received for tuition I now entertained them no longer."

According to Totten's journal, in the early 1850s student costs at William and Mary averaged about $196 per year: a $20 ticket fee for each class; $5 deposit; $5 matriculation fee; $3 room rent; $120 for board, washing, fuel, and lights; and $3 for a servant's fee for slaves to shine boots and clean shoes, sweep rooms and carry firewood and fresh water to the rooms twice a day.

Students continued to play pranks and were frequently disorderly. Totten noted that often students "would rise at midnight, break open the belfry door and ring the College bell furiously." Lacking management experience, Johns drew upon Totten's past presidential experience to help him administer the college, and the Totten family moved into The Brafferton in 1851, so he might better help maintain order and assume the post of president of the faculty in Bishop John's absence.

Johns resigned as president March 31, 1854, moving to Alexandria. In 1862, upon the death of Bishop Meade, he become the fourth bishop of Virginia. Totten believed he would succeed Johns as president, but the bishop recommended mathematics professor Ewell. About this time a letter in a Richmond newspaper accused Totten of a "lack of sympathy with Southern Institutions." Both the faculty and students publicly denied the allegation, but the damage was done and the visitors voted for Ewell.

Totten was not fond of Ewell, whom he described as "captious, unreasonable and tyrannical," but Ewell was popular with the students and townspeople because "he would stoop to anything to get their good will." Totten's description was far from "Old Buck," Ewell's conscientious and dedicated professor image, commonly applied to him in later years by others. However, Ewell served as president (from 1854-1888) longer than any president except Blair and Madison. When he retired he was named president emeritus.

Ewell exerted much effort in trying to build up the college; in 1855 he published its first general catalogue, which was enlarged in 1859. In 1856-1857 the college building was extensively repaired and changed, with the front portico widened and lecture rooms painted and refitted. The historic Blue Room remained as it was, "decorated with its historical portraits, etc.," and the third floor was entirely transformed with the "rude arches" and "corpulent chimneys" pulled down and flooring relaid for more convenient dormitory space. The Williamsburg *Weekly Gazette* on July 8, 1857, reported that old students would not recognize the interior of the building.

Unfortunately, on February 8, 1859, the main building was destroyed by fire. According to Totten's report, signed by Ewell, the fire started in the north wing, either in the chemical laboratory or in the basement under it. In short order all the building's woodwork and chimneys were destroyed along with at least 8,000 library books, including in part the gifts of kings, archbishops, bishops, nobles, colonial governors, and the assembly. The library was situated in the north wing, where the "Great Hall" is now located.

Professor Robert J. Morrison wrote of the fire: "I had not reached the College when I met President Ewell, who had just returned from the second floor of the building, where he had been to rescue the students who were sleeping in the dormitories. . . . Soon the citizens of Williamsburg flocked to the sad scene. Ladies and gentlemen were silent, sorrowful spectators of the ravages of

From the drawing book of Mary F. Southall came these views of the east side of the college building and the rear (west side) in July, 1856. Just three years later the building was nearly destroyed by fire. The uses of the building's rooms have been labeled in the drawing of the rear elevation. Courtesy of the College Archives, College of William and Mary

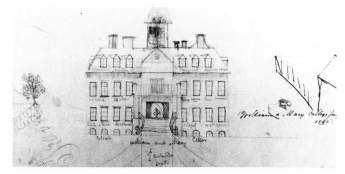

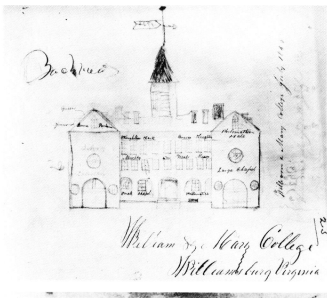

The third version of the Sir Christopher Wren Building is shown in this lithograph. The third building, with twin Italianate towers, was built in late 1859 and remained until the fire of September, 1862. This picture shows a roadway running parallel to the structure. Such a roadway is not described elsewhere in college accounts of the day. Courtesy of the College Archives, College of William and Mary

An old watercolor painting shows the results of the February 8, 1859 fire, which severely damaged the Sir Christopher Wren Building. The Brafferton, untouched by the flames, stands at the left. Note that only the outer walls are left standing to the tops of the second-floor windows. Courtesy of the Richmond Times-Dispatch; Thomas L. Williams photo

The program for the commencement exercises of July 4, 1860 lists only two graduates that year: J. Filmer Hubbard and Thomas Jefferson Stubbs, who returned to his alma mater later in the century as a professor. Courtesy of the College Archives, College of William and Mary

COMMENCEMENT EXERCISES

OF THE

College of William and Mary,

JULY 4TH 1860.

Music.

PRAYER BY THE RIGHT REV. BISHOP JOHNS.

Music.

Oration by THOS. JEFFERSON STUBBS, A. B., of Gloucester.

Music.

NAMES OF GRADUATES.

J. FILMER HUBBARD, A. B.

THOS. JEFFERSON STUBBS, A. B.

Announcement of the names of Students entitled to Certificates of Proficiency.

The Conferring of Degrees.

Music.

Address to the Students, by JAMES LYONS, ESQ., of Richmond, Va.

Music.

Address before the Society of ALUMNI, by GEO. WYTHE MUNFORD, Secretary of the Commonwealth.

Music.

Poem before the PHI BETA KAPPA Society, by Dr. THOS. DUNN ENGLISH, of Va.

Music.

The Exercises will commence at 11 o'clock, A. M., in the College Chapel. The public are invited to attend.

A drawing by L. J. Cranstone depicts the college grounds between 1860 and 1862 as seen from the Richmond Road side of campus. The President's House is on the left and the college with its large twin Italianate towers is in the middle. This third version of the Sir Christopher Wren Building lasted only about three years before fire again nearly destroyed the structure. Courtesy of the Colonial Williamsburg Foundation

Here is another view of the third building which was erected on the surviving walls of the old main structure after the fire of February 8, 1859. The twin Italianate towers distinguish the building from its predecessor and successor. This building was destroyed on September 9, 1862 by a fire started by Union troops. Courtesy of the College Archives, College of William and Mary; Richmond Times-Dispatch photo

the flames. Any attempt to stay their progress would have been vain. The records of the college were saved, as well as the old portraits that hung in the Blue Room. The President saved the college seal..."

Also lost during the fire was the scientific apparatus, some of which was nearly 100 years old and had been selected by Dr. William Small. An 1859 newspaper account of the fire noted that nothing remained "of the venerable Alma Mater but its smoking ruins...The large building...is said to have been constructed from a design by Sir Christopher Wren...but its architectural merits were by no means worthy of this great master mechanic. It was of no style, and had no redeeming quality but its natural durability."

Durable the building was. On March 1, 1859, at a regular meeting of the faculty, consideration was given to a proposal to rebuild the college utilizing the old walls. A student meeting the next day lamented the destruction. The student resolution said, "We hold any individual loss we may have sustained, whether of effects or by the temporary interruption of our studies, as far subordinate to the loss to our country of such a valuable historic monument."

The college building was insured for more than $20,000. The surviving walls were examined by expert bricklayers, who assured the committee that the walls, which contained more than 1,250,000 bricks, were "strong enough for a warehouse," and could not be "pulled down without a very great destruction of bricks." The bricklayers added that "it would be wasteful extravagance to pull them down and build new ones." Rebuilding was accomplished in short order, but the building had a completely different appearance, with twin towers in the front built "of the Italian style of Architecture." The building was ready to reopen in October 1859, and Dr. William Barton Rogers, former professor at William and Mary and later president of the Massachusetts Institute of Technology, assisted in replacing the philosophical and chemical apparatus. By 1860 the library, "selected with great care," consisted of "nearly 5,000 volumes" and more than seventy students were enrolled in classes.

Former United States President John Tyler, who had been a member of the visitors since the early 1820s and had remained on the board while he was United States president, had been rector since 1848, and in 1859 the college named him chancellor as well, the first American chancellor since George Washington.

Although the college was restored, by May 1861, the War Between the States had erupted and Virginia was threatened with immediate invasion. Classes were suspended, and the president, students, and professors left, many joining the Confederate Army. Ewell, a unionist, believed secession was unconstitutional, but he later organized the Thirty-second Virginia Infantry and became its colonel at age fifty-one.

The main college building was used by the Confederate military, first as a barracks and later as a hospital, until May, 1862, when the Battle of Williamsburg was fought. The Union troops, led by General George B. McClellan, moved up the Virginia peninsula from Fort Monroe in late April, and on May 5 fought on the outskirts of Williamsburg with Confederate troops commanded by General Joseph E. Johnston. The city fell under Union control as Southern forces withdrew.

Confederate forces returned on September 9, 1862, and raided the city, driving the Union troops to the east for just one day; thirty-three Union soldiers who were sleeping on the lawn at the college were captured. Later that afternoon the college building was burned, and one eyewitness stated that some of the Fifth Pennsylvania Cavalry "surrounded the building with drawn swords to prevent any attempt at extinguishing the fire." Some people felt the Union soldiers burned the building to keep Confederate snipers from using it. Union troops commanded the streets for the remainder of the war.

Ewell returned to Williamsburg after the war. On July 5, 1865, he reported to the visitors meeting in Richmond that the remaining walls of the college were "apparently in as good condition as they were after the fire of 1859, in fact are less warped and cracked." Much of the library and scientific equipment was saved from the fire because it had been moved to the Eastern Lunatic Asylum when the Southern forces withdrew. Later the statue of Lord Botetourt also was moved to the asylum grounds. Estimated war losses were $70,000 to the main building, about $3,000 in damages to The Brafferton and $1,600 in damages to the President's House.

When the college reopened in October 1865, classes were conducted in The Brafferton, with eighteen college students and thirty-two grammar school boys attending; a wing had been added to the President's House to accommodate professors. On July 10, 1868, the faculty, however, voted to

WILLIAM & MARY COLLEGE. WILLIAMSBURG.   USED AS A HOSPITAL.

In this illustration of the college front campus, note the reference to the building "used as a hospital." Confederate forces used it as a hospital until the Battle of Williamsburg on May 5, 1862, when Union forces took over the town. A wooden fence has been placed around the statue of Lord Botetourt, apparently for protection. Courtesy of William A. Molineux

This completely distorted view of Williamsburg was drawn by a Union soldier in 1862. The asylum is on the far left with the towers; the powder magazine is in the center with the pointed roof; and the college is in the upper right corner with its twin towers. Woodcut from The Story of the 33rd New York State Volunteers

This rough drawing of the college campus was made after the Battle of Williamsburg on May 5, 1862, and the town's takeover by Union troops. A United States flag has been drawn on a pole in the middle of the front yard. There is little other evidence that a flag pole was actually located there. Note the clutter of war in the bottom of the drawing—broken wagons and debris. From Battles and Leaders of the Civil War, *Vol. 2*

WILLIAM AND MARY COLLEGE, VIRGINIA.

The rear of the main college building is shown in 1862, prior to the fire of September 9, 1862. A United States flag has been placed in the corner of the lithograph, obviously to note occupation of the college campus by Union forces, which took over Williamsburg on May 5, 1862 and remained in charge until 1865. The illustration was originally printed in Frank Leslie's Illustrated Newspaper on March 10, 1866. From the author's collection

The main college building was burned by Union soldiers on September 9, 1862. This drawing, by Major Edward Cronin of the Union Army, apparently depicts Confederate cavalry attacking Union soldiers defending the campus. Courtesy of the New York Historical Society

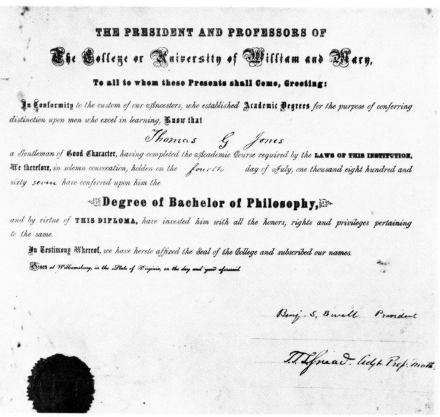

The diploma of Thomas G. Jones, dated July 4, 1867, shows that Latin was not used then and that the document had taken on a somewhat modern look. It was labelled "The College or University of William and Mary." It was signed by "Benj. S. Ewell, president" and "T.T.L. Snead, Adjt Prof: Math." Courtesy of the College Archives, College of William and Mary; Thomas L. Williams photo

Historian Hugh Blair Grigsby of Norfolk served as chancellor of William and Mary from 1871 to 1881. Courtesy of the College Archives, College of William and Mary

In October 1869, college students gather around the new main building, the fourth building to use the original walls. Designed by Alfred Rives of Richmond, at the time of this picture, it was ready for classroom use. Note the residue from construction around the structure. Courtesy of the Colonial Williamsburg Foundation

suspend college classes until the main building could be rebuilt and the other college facilities repaired. Plans were being drawn to rebuild the college building, again within its original walls; the new building was ready for use in October 1869. For the rebuilding, Ewell worked hard to obtain contributions from many Virginians, the archbishop of Canterbury and others in England, and individuals along the East Coast.

Ewell tried three times, appearing before committees of the United States Congress, to secure payments from the government for damages suffered by the college during the war. But all his efforts failed and it was not until 1893 that partial indemnification was secured. In 1871 a "commodious brick buliding" had been erected for the grammar and Matty School "near the foundations of the old Palace."

The war had stripped the South of its economy and the ravaged communities struggled to survive. Such was the case at Williamsburg and the college. By July 1881, William and Mary had only twelve students and the next year there were just three "true" students and two professors. Ewell recommended to the visitors that they ask the Virginia General Assembly to take over and fund the college as a state normal school, primarily designed to train teachers. The college property at that time was valued at $130,000; the main building, at $65,000.

In July 1882, minutes of the visitors report that the college "shall be continued for the reception and education of students" for the 1882-1883 year, but there were virtually no students in attendance and college exercises were suspended. The buildings were carefully maintained and the school's debts reduced by various financial means, including renting various rooms.

According to college tradition, the ringing of the college bell by Ewell during the "silent years" from 1882 to 1888 maintained the royal charter and kept the college alive.

The Boston Christian Register, on September 23, 1886, reported that Edwin D. Head, in his recent "Old South" lecture, spoke about William and Mary: "The old, gray-haired President (Ewell), as each October comes round, goes to the college, and has the college bell rung, as a formality to still retain the charter...[the] president, with whom I talked there in these last May days, believes that the bell will yet be heard.

"It is a pity when one considers the educational needs of the South, that something should

This photograph of the college front yard, with the main building (center), The Brafferton (left) and the President's House (right) was apparently taken between 1869 and 1875. Note the absence of the statue of Lord Botetourt in the front yard; it was removed to Eastern State Hospital for safe keeping, sometime about September, 1864, and believed returned to the campus in 1874. Note the students wandering inside the fence which fronts Jamestown Road. Courtesy of the Colonial Williamsburg Foundation

This is the only known view of the statue of Lord Botetourt when it stood on the grounds of Eastern State Hospital, between about 1864 and 1874. Courtesy of the Colonial Williamsburg Foundation

not be done to perpetuate this old college, second only to Harvard in age and historical interest, both in memory of its great past and in active service of the present. Such great traditions as those of William and Mary College are themselves of the highest utility in education and ought not to be wasted."

(Ewell on January 19, 1887, in a letter to Professor Herbert B. Adams, associate professor of history at Johns Hopkins University, said about the bell: "There is an ancient tradition connected with the college to the effect that a full session of students followed the ringing of its bell on the 1st of October at sunrise. The session began early in October. The transformation of this tradition into a daily ringing by me exceeds the story of the 'Three Black Crows.' But, to compensate, it has given me a wide reputation as a 'bell-ringer,' equal or superior to that of the celebrated 'Swiss bell-ringers.' So I laugh at the story without murmuring

A rare photograph shows the William and Mary faculty in 1873. From left to right are L. B. Wharton, Benjamin Stoddert Ewell (president), Thomas T. L. Snead (standing), George T. Wilmer, Richard A. Wise (standing with hand inside coat), and Charles S. Dodd. Courtesy of the College Archives, College of William and Mary

Professors of Wm & Mary College

1 L.B. Wharton, 2 Pres. B.S. Ewell 3 T.T.L. Snead 4 Dr. Wilmer
5 Rich'd A. Wise 6. J. Morgan Smethic

This is the current college bell in the cupola of the Sir Christopher Wren Building. A bell has called students to class since students were first on campus nearly 290 years ago. College President Benjamin Stoddert Ewell was called "the old bell ringer," because legend says he rang the bell to open every session, even while the college was closed between 1881 and 1888. This bell, placed in the cupola in 1889, was rung by hand until September 1976, when it was electrified. It is now rung by pushing a button. On Senior Day, the last day of classes, seniors are allowed to ring the bell constantly and the old rope is used again. Courtesy of the Associated Press

The Wise Light Infantry poses on June 29, 1875, in front of the Sir Christopher Wren Building. The troop was organized by Professor Richard Alsop Wise (front row, center, with beard) and consisted of college students and townspeople. Note the apparent sad condition of the building with broken windows above the door behind the group. Courtesy of the College Archives, College of William and Mary

In 1875-1876, many students boarded anywhere they could in town. This group lived at the Wythe House on Palace Green. The photograph was taken in front of the Wren Building. Courtesy of the College Archives, College of William and Mary

or contradicting.")

On March 5, 1888, the general assembly finally enacted a bill providing for the reorganization and rehabilitation of "this old institution." The act provided for $10,000 annually to be appropriated for the college, "which shall establish a system of normal instruction and training." It also required that the college board of visitors consist of the existing ten members and additional "associate visitors, who shall be appointed by the governor."

President Ewell's final report to the visitors was made on May 10, 1888. He stated that although the college was reopening, he could not handle the task at age sixty-eight. The visitors decided the next day, and, according to the minutes, elected Dr. John L. Buchanan of Richmond (vice president of the visitors and state superintendent of public instruction) as the next president. However, he was not at the meeting and a committee was appointed to notify him of his selection and to obtain his decision on whether to accept the appointment. Buchanan asked for some time to consider the matter.

On July 5, 1888, Dr. Buchanan notified the board that he could not accept the appointment as college president, and on August 23 the visitors named Lyon G. Tyler, son of United States President John Tyler, the new college president. Tyler had received his B.A. and M.A. degrees from the University of Virginia and had previously taught at William and Mary in 1877-1878, as professor of *belles lettres*, leaving to become a high school principal in Memphis, Tennessee. Returning to Richmond in 1882 to practice law, Tyler established the Virginia Mechanics' Institute night school, where he taught. He also was elected to the House of Delegates and helped push through the legislature the bill establishing the college as a state male normal school.

The nineteenth century painting of Benjamin Stoddert Ewell, William and Mary president from 1854 to 1888, has recently been restored and hangs in the presidents' gallery on the second floor of the Sir Christopher Wren Building. Courtesy of the College Art Collection, College of William and Mary

President Benjamin Stoddert Ewell and Professor Hugh Stockdell Bird (right), the youngest professor, were photographed in 1888. The two men were seated in the library, which at the time was located in the rear of the chapel, in the southeast corner of the old main building. Courtesy of the College Archives, College of William and Mary

In 1859, the president and faculty laid off land to "the rear of the president's garden" as a "burying ground for the professors of the college, their families, and the students" to be called "The College Cemetery." It stands today between George Preston Blow Gymnasium and Chancellors Hall (formerly Rogers Hall). President Benjamin Stoddert Ewell is buried there. Courtesy of the Richmond Times-Dispatch

The interior of the chapel in the main building is shown about 1888. The man standing in the center under the chandelier is Benjamin Stoddert Ewell, college president from 1854 to 1888. Courtesy of the Colonial Williamsburg Foundation

Chapter Nine
1888-1919
Tyler Revives the College's Fortunes

yon Gardiner Tyler succeeded to the William and Mary presidency at the end of an era, but also at the culmination of a plan designed by Benjamin S. Ewell to save the old school. Ewell's custody of the college was completed and the general assembly had finally approved his plan, which would provide annual state funds that would lead to a revival of the "sinking fortunes of the institution."

Russell T. Smith, in his manuscript, *Distinctive Traditions at the College of William and Mary and Their Influence on the Modernization of the College, 1865-1919*, wrote that the new students attending the school were largely drawn "from a lower socioeconomic level than the other Virginia colleges in order that they be prepared for careers as public school teachers and administrators." The effectiveness of teacher training at the college is attested in an 1898 report which called William and Mary, "the right arm of the public school system." Legislators, while willing to give the

"The Seven Wise Men" comprised the entire faculty in 1888. From left to right are: standing—Hugh S. Bird, professor of pedagogy; Thomas Jefferson Stubbs, professor of mathematics; and Charles Edward Bishop, professor of Greek, French, and German. Seated—the Reverend Lyman B. Wharton, professor of Latin; Lyon Gardiner Tyler, college president; Van Franklin Garrett, professor of natural science; and John Leslie Hall, professor of English and history. Courtesy of the Society of the Alumni

school some funds, were unwilling to increase public support for education. "Similarly, many private philanthropists in the Old Dominion probably found the lower class connotations of the college public school connection unattractive," Smith wrote.

Therefore, Tyler found himself in a difficult financial situation, like many of his predecessors; nevertheless, he was able to attract a highly capable faculty, "The Seven Wise Men," as they have been called. Tyler, who was later to receive a number of honorary doctoral degrees, also served as professor of moral science, political economy, and civil government while president. His faculty included Dr. J. Leslie Hall, professor of English language; Thomas Jefferson Stubbs, professor of mathematics; the Reverend Lyman B. Wharton, professor of ancient and modern languages; Dr. Van F. Garrett, professor of natural science; and Hugh S. Bird, professor of methods and pedagogics. Most of these men remained at the school for many years, though some professorships occasionally varied.

By 1890, there were 104 students registered at the college, and for the next twenty years literary societies, which had flourished from the 1830s to 1860, had been revived. The Phoenix and Philomathean literary societies now regularly had forty students each. The two organizations produced the first literary magazine, *The William and Mary College Monthly*, the first student-run publication at the college. It contained a collection of student essays, fiction, and verse.

Considered by many to be a good historian and author, Tyler developed, in July 1892, the first edition of what he called the *William and*

Mary College Quarterly Historical Magazine, now called the *William and Mary Quarterly,* the oldest Southern historic magazine still in existence. Initially, Tyler published it as a private venture under the auspices of the college but now the publication is part of The Institute of Early American History and Culture at the college, sponsored by William and Mary and the Colonial Williamsburg Foundation.

In 1893, the college celebrated its 200th anniversary with a major program which took place on June 21. An anniversary oration was presented by J. Allen Watts of Roanoke and an alumni banquet was held. The five-day celebration was held in association with the end of the session and graduation exercises.

Also during the bicentennial year, another Ewell effort finally bore fruit. The United States Congress finally agreed to partially indemnify the college for losses during the Revolutionary and Civil wars and $64,000 was received. Student enrollment continued to increase, with many of the students attending tuition-free under state regulations that called for them to teach in the public schools for two years upon graduation.

On November 11, 1893, William and Mary fielded its first football team, which played the Norfolk Y.M.C.A. team. The college lost, 16-0. The first intercollegiate football game was played November 10, 1894, with Hampden-Sydney College winning, 24-0.

The governance of the college was quite difficult, especially under the design formulated by the legislature. There was a group of ten visitors who, through perpetual appointments, succeeded from the original charter visitors; then there was the new group of ten visitors appointed by the governor. At the time of the general assembly legislation, Judge W. W. Crump of Richmond, rector of the college since 1883, was elected "president" of the newly arranged board. In 1892, Crump retired and General William B. Taliaferro, a board member and educator who had worked tirelessly to help get the college bill through the legislature, was the elected rector and president. However, the battles among the old visitors and the new group intensified and in 1892, according to board minutes, the charter group decided to elect Colonel William B. Lamb of Norfolk as rector, while Taliaferro remained as board president.

This double board continued for the next fourteen years with both groups lobbying for support among alumni and legislators. Lamb fought many

of the reforms proposed by Tyler and the other board members. In 1898, Taliaferro died and Dr. John W. Lawson, of Isle of Wight County, was elected board president. He served until 1905, when Robert Morton Hughes of Norfolk was elected president. Later, in 1906, the general assembly enacted legislation which made William and Mary a "true" state institution and reorganized the board of visitors, with ten members appointed by the governor and with the state superintendent of public instruction as an ex-officio voting member.

In 1906, Lamb, the oldest board member and the senior member in point of service, was not reappointed by the governor, in an effort to eliminate the major point of contention among the visitors, and Hughes was elected rector. Therefore, between 1890-1906, Lawson was the only principal officer of the board never to carry the historic title of rector.

Delighted by the general assembly's actions to make the college a complete state institution, on June 12, 1906, Tyler reported to the visitors: "The time came, when the Phoenix of old, risen from its ashes, was arranged in plumage more attractive than it has ever before possessed." Nearly 200 years earlier, Hugh Jones, recalling the college fire of 1705 in his work, *The Present State of Virginia,* also described the college as "Phoenix-like as the City of London, revived and improved out of its own ruins."

In 1894, board member Thomas H. Barnes, in a candid observation of Tyler, said, "I like Tyler and give him credit for his literary attainments and for his qualifications and fitness for the place he occupies as president...but I have long since been impressed with his lack of financial grip and with his wild and extravagant notions...." However, Barnes acknowledged that he and other board members had given Tyler carte blanche in financial matters. The board began to exert influence in the spending, but Tyler found no interference in his designs to raise money and increase the school's endowment.

By 1907, the college's endowment had grown to $154,000, up from $20,000 in 1888. (Before the Civil War, the endowment in 1861 was about $158,000.) Funds from the state had increased annually to $35,000 from the initial $10,000. Tyler's report continued that there were ten buildings "all in fine condition, well equipped, lighted with electricity, and supplied with the purest sort of water from an artesian well." The library had grown from 7,000 volumes in 1888 to approximately 15,000, and the corps of instructors numbered twenty-five, when at no time in the history of the school before 1888 had the professors exceeded ten. The student body numbered over 200, the most by that time in the college's history.

In the 1961 *Alumni Gazette,* alumnus E.J. Cooley (1900) recalled arriving at William and Mary in 1898 and finding President Tyler "hard at work in his shirt sleeves." Cooley and his brother, E. M. Cooley, paid the registrar $10 each for one month's board, lodging, and laundry. College opened, he recalled, with all the professors and ministers of the town seated on "the stage" for chapel exercises with about 200 students waiting in their pews for instructions and devotions. Cooley wrote about the "excellent courses" he had under Tyler, Hall, Garrett, Stubbs, and the other Wise Men.

Tyler worked hard to strengthen the authority of the administration, which was, at this point, a very feeble organization. The administration would not be fully developed until the 1920s, partly because of the domination of the college power structure by Rector Hughes, who assumed authority not previously vested with the visitors. The rector oversaw most new construction, gave advice on the investment of college funds, approved requests of professors for leaves of absence, controlled details of architectural style, and at times modified the menu of the college boardinghouse.

The regime of Hughes ended in 1918, when Governor Westmoreland Davis failed to reappoint most of the Hughes faction to the board. Tyler described the 1905-1918 Hughes era, noting "the idea of tying the hands of the President was persisted in until the new board, under Westmoreland Davis came on, who I found, believed in vesting the President with proper authority."

Many of Tyler's fund-raising efforts concentrated on securing money from a number of charitable foundations, such as the Peabody, Ogden, and Rockefeller foundations. Unfortunately, they were unsuccessful for the most part, sometimes because of Tyler's approach and at other times because leadership at other colleges, when asked about William and Mary, did not offer favorable comments. The Carnegie Foundation did give the college one $20,000 grant toward the construction of a new library, but the University of Virginia in the same year received $100,000 from the Rockefeller Foundation to endow a new department of education.

A youthful Lyon Gardiner Tyler, an attorney in Richmond, came to William and Mary as president in 1888. Born in Charles City County, in 1853, Tyler was the son of United States President John Tyler and his wife Julia Gardiner Tyler. Courtesy of the Office of University Communications, College of William and Mary

Tyler felt the best way to restore William and Mary to its rightful position of influence among institutions of higher education was to promote the college's heritage, reciting and recalling the fact that many of the patriots who led the American Revolution attended the school, and recalling the leadership aims and priorities of the college through the centuries. His emphasis on history and his own literary efforts encouraged students to involve themselves further in publication efforts. *The Colonial Echo,* the college's yearbook, was begun in 1899 with a 200-page edition, and on October 3, 1911, the first issue of the student newspaper, *The Flat Hat,* appeared with headlines proclaiming the college "begins 219th year" and "Football Team at Regular Practice."

Two events in the final eighteen months of the Tyler administration played major roles in the future prosperity of the college: Governor Davis

showed a personal interest in improving the school, and William and Mary became the first senior institution in Virginia to admit women.

By 1917, William and Mary seemed on the road to recovery, but World War I suddenly brought a 25 percent decline in enrollment. In 1918, the general assembly passed an act and Tyler was persuaded to admit women in order to maintain a viable number of students. "Tyler planned carefully for the arrival of women in the fall [of 1918] and the new dean of women showed her sensitivity to college customs by urging the women to 'establish a tradition' rather than framing a stringent set of regulations to govern their conduct," Russel T. Smith wrote.

In 1919, however, Tyler was sixty-six years old and had been president of William and Mary for thirty-two years; retirement sounded good to him. Like his predecessor Ewell, Tyler retired with the honorary title of president emeritus. Tyler retired to his home, Lion's Den, in Charles City County, where he began publication of *Tyler's Quarterly Historical Magazine*. He died on February 12, 1935.

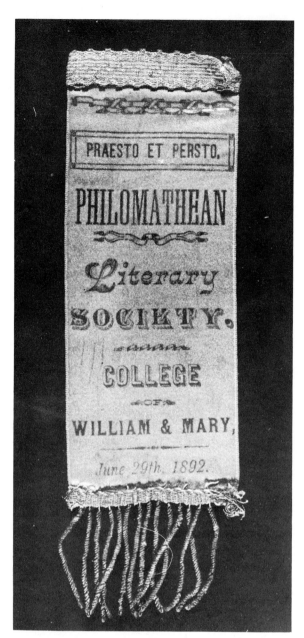

A Richmond photographer, J. H. Stone, took this "Bird's Eye View" of William and Mary about 1890. The students have gathered in the yard fronting Jamestown Road. Courtesy of the Colonial Williamsburg Foundation

In the early 1890s students gathered in the front yard for a visiting photographer. Note the details in the statue of Lord Botetourt, which now have become worn or have vanished because of years of exposure to the elements. Courtesy of the Colonial Williamsburg Foundation

In the mid-1890s, the college was concentrated around the colonial yard, with related facilities along Jamestown Road. This is a rear view of the Sir Christopher Wren Building (center); notice that the great hall wing had been converted into two floors and the great round windows on the end had been bricked up. Courtesy of the College Archives, College of William and Mary

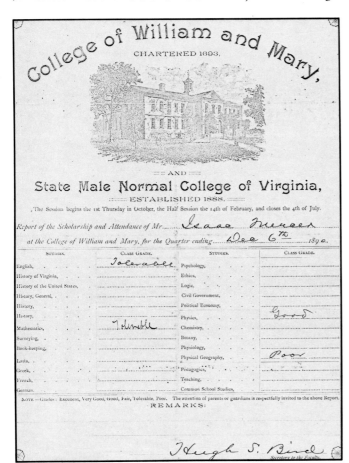

This is a copy of the report of scholarship and attendance of an Isaac Mercer who attended William and Mary in the fall of 1890. The document was signed by Hugh S. Bird, who was secretary to the faculty. Courtesy of J. Wilfred Lambert

William and Mary fielded its first football team in 1893, with H. G. Humphrey as the team captain. There were three games during the season. The first game was against the Norfolk YMCA and the college lost, 16-0. However, the season ended with two wins against Capital City A. C. (6-4), and against the Old Dominion Club (14-4). The first intercollegiate football game was in 1894 against Hampden-Sydney College; William and Mary lost, 24-0. Courtesy of the College Archives, College of William and Mary

In 1896 the entire student body posed in front of the Sir Christopher Wren Building. Notice the hairstyles—many of them parted their hair down the middle—and the clothing styles. Most students wore a suit with vest, white shirt, and tie to classes. *Courtesy of the College Archives, College of William and Mary*

In 1852, the College Hotel was built across Jamestown Road to house the college steward, who had formerly used The Brafferton. After the college reopened in October 1865, and while the main building was still in ruins, President Benjamin Ewell noted that the College Hotel was large enough to accommodate the steward's family and at least twenty boarders, and provide one or two "recitation rooms." The building later was used as a women's dormitory and called Ewell Hall, the first of several buildings to honor Ewell. Courtesy of the College Archives, College of William and Mary

Members of the Philomathean Literary Society pose in front of the Sir Christopher Wren Building for a photograph to be published in the first yearbook in 1899. Courtesy of the College Archives, College of William and Mary

This is a photograph of the Annual Alumni Banquet on June 27, 1897. The site of the gathering is unknown. Courtesy of the College Archives, College of William and Mary

At the turn of the century, the Taliaferro Building (center) and the College Infirmary (far right) were located beside Ewell Hall (porch at far left). The Taliaferro Building was transformed into the fine arts department in the late 1930s and was torn down about 1967. Courtesy of the College Archives, College of William and Mary

Tennis has been a popular pastime and sport at William and Mary for at least ninety years. This 1899-1900 photograph shows the twenty-five members of the Tennis Club with rackets in hand. The club was one of several sports clubs for the gentlemen on campus. Courtesy of the College Archives, College of William and Mary

The first theatrical production at William and Mary probably occurred in 1702, but records are scanty and the eighteenth century college theatre is hardly more than legendary. By 1900, however, there had been numerous productions on campus and there was a Paint and Powder Club which routinely presented plays. This is a photograph from an unnamed production. From left to right, the cast was James B. Thomas; Edwin B. Hutchinson; Thomas Jefferson Stubbs, Jr.; Harry L. Hundley, Jr.; Robert Frederick Saunders; John G. Anderson; Fairfax Shields Macandlish; John Beverly Booneville; and Robert Morton Hughes, Jr. Courtesy of the College Archives, College of William and Mary

The first student publication at the college was the William and Mary College Monthly. The editorial staff in 1899-1900 included, from left to right, John Taylor Thompson, James Hunt, Curtis Gresham, John Munford Coles, Harry A. Hurt, Donald Hebditch, and J. Howard Bonneville. Courtesy of the College Archives, College of William and Mary

Jamestown Road was still a wide dirt path about 1900. The Brafferton was used as a dormitory and shutters had been added. A sturdy white fence enclosed the college yard. A stile at the fence was used instead of a gate. Courtesy of the College Archives, College of William and Mary

The priorities of William and Mary were formulated by college president Lyon G. Tyler about 1900. This listing is on a plaque situated on the back wall of the Sir Christopher Wren Building. At least one additional priority has been uncovered. In 1779, William and Mary became the first college to include the study of fine arts in its curriculum. The professorship of Robert Andrews was changed during the "Jefferson reorganization" to include fine arts as part of his coursework. Courtesy of the Office of University Communications, College of William and Mary

POWDER·MAGAZINE (1716).

PRESIDENT'S HOUSE, WILLIAM AND MARY COLLEGE.

A drawing of the President's House about the turn of the century reveals the porch added in 1848-1849 and the addition (at left) built in 1865 to accommodate professors while the main building was in ruins. A large front porch also had been added, with a picket fence in the front as well as the familiar fence at the rear. Courtesy of the Colonial Williamsburg Foundation

PRIORITIES
OF THE COLLEGE OF WILLIAM AND MARY.

Chartered February 8, 1693, by King William and Queen Mary. Main building designed by Sir Christopher Wren.

FIRST College in the United States in its antecedents, which go back to the College proposed at Henrico (1619). Second to Harvard University in actual operation.

FIRST American College to receive its charter from the Crown under the Seal of the Privy Council, 1693. Hence it was known as "their Majesties' Royal College of William and Mary."

FIRST and ONLY American College to receive a Coat-of-Arms from the College of Heralds, 1694.

FIRST College in the United States to have a full Faculty, consisting of a President, six Professors, usher, and writing master, 1729.

FIRST College to confer medallic prizes: the gold medals donated by Lord Botetourt in 1771.

FIRST College to establish an inter-collegiate fraternity, the Phi Beta Kappa, December 5, 1776.

FIRST College to have the Elective System of study, 1779.

FIRST College to have the Honor System, 1779.

FIRST College to become a University, 1779.

FIRST College to have a school of Modern Languages, 1779.

FIRST College to have a school of Municipal and Constitutional Law, 1779.

FIRST College to teach Political Economy, 1784.

FIRST College to have a school of Modern History, 1803.

Presented by the Colonial Capital Branch of
The Association for the
Preservation of Virginia Antiquities,
1914.

Five nattily-dressed students pose in the college front yard about 1900 with the statue of Lord Botetourt and the Sir Christopher Wren Building in the background. Courtesy of the Colonial Williamsburg Foundation

Members of the 1904 football team are shown on the field during the first game of the year against Norfolk High School. William and Mary won, 18-0. From the 1905 Colonial Echo

Students who lived in The Brafferton had their own campus club called the Brafferton Indians. In appropriate attire the members posed for the 1906 yearbook. From the 1906 Colonial Echo

Members of the William and Mary Track Team of 1908-1909 model the latest in athletic uniforms. Notice the cleats on some of the shoes. Courtesy of the College Archives, College of William and Mary

THE FLAT HAT

VOL. I.   COLLEGE OF WILLIAM AND MARY IN VIRGINIA   No. 1

WILLIAM AND MARY BEGINS 219th YEAR

A Large Registration and Many Improvements

William and Mary, the time-honored alma mater of so many illustrious men, began its two hundred and nineteenth session on Thursday, September 21, under circumstances the most auspicious in its history. Until Saturday noon the total number of registrants was 175, an unusually large number so early in the session. Students, old and new, continue to arrive, and as we go to press there are many men about the campus who have not registered. Judging from past years it may be reasonably expected that fifty or more will enter the College before the close of the session.

Throughout the past summer many improvements have been made about the campus. Lecture rooms have been newly painted, worn out apparatus replaced by new, and the dormitories refurnished. Shortly after the opening of the session a committee from the Board of Visitors came here, and, after a thorough inspection of college conditions

Scrubs 0. Invincibles 0

On Saturday while the varsity was engaged in vainly trying to stem the tide among the green, vine clad hills of Albemarle, the Scrubs with head and nose knee deep in sand plunged, replunged and plunged again for the glory of alma mater on Cary Field. It was a case of an invincible force striking an immovable substance, for grovel as they might, sneeze and cough out signals no matter how quickly, neither side could score. The nearest approaches to it were when Geddy narrowly missed a drop kick and again when English made a fifty yard run only to be called back for stepping outside. Rowe for the scrubs came very near getting through the line once but something happened and the Invincibles got the ball. Cogbill played a beautiful game for the Invincibles. Healy played well for scrubs. Line up:

Scrubs.		Invincibles.
Healy	c	Mitchell
Wright, E. S.	r. g	Harrison
Nourse	r. t	Clements
Mayor	r. e	Witchley
Sommers	r. g	Wright, G.
Bane	l. t	Cox
Turner	l. e	Garth
Hall	f. b	Cogbill
Rowe	l. h	Thomas
Brooks	r. h	English
Jackson	q. b	Geddy

Annual Y. M. C. A. Reception

On the night of Tuesday, Sept. 26, the Y. M. C. A. tendered its annual reception to the new students and friends of this institution, and if the attendance and the evident good will be considered as indications, we predict a remarkable record for the Y. M. C. A. this year.

The reception was presided over by President H. W. Vaden aided by the Y. M. C. A. cabinet. Rev. Mr. Hoover, of the Baptist church, and the Rev. E. Ruffin Jones, of Bruton Parish church, delivered short and helpful talks, as did the President, Mr. Vaden, and Dr. Keeble. Dr. Wilson spoke on the Honor System, the pride of William and Mary, and Dr. Young in a brief talk brought forth the many-sidedness of college spirit.

Messrs. James and Deierhoi spoke in behalf of their literary societies, Philomathean and Phoenix respectively. During the course of the evening THE FLAT HAT was ably introduced by the editor-in-chief, William Kavanaugh Doty, and its aims and objects explained. Refreshments were served, and the pleasantest Y. M. C. A. reception ever held at William and Mary came to an end, having been materially brightened by the presence of the Institute teachers and students.

FOOTBALL TEAM AT REGULAR PRACTICE

New Coach Employing Best Methods

Football practice has been going on now for a week and the fellows ought to have gotten a line on the team by this time. One thing is evident, that green bunch that went out on Cary Field is being gotten into shape by Dr. Young about as fast as possible and while there is nothing very heavy about the team, they will, with grit and headwork render an account of themselves that William and Mary will be proud of.

This year a new factor has arisen which has caused quite a good deal of loss to the team. This factor is the ruling out of men in the "prep" classes. Heretofore they have been allowed to play and the men recruited from these lower ranks were the best on the team and this has been so, for years back. This year however they have been eliminated and as a consequence, many a hefty prospect roams over the campus, the cynosure of envious eyes. This ren-

The William and Mary student newspaper, The Flat Hat, *was first published on October 3, 1911, as a four-column by ten-inch paper. Through an error, the founding date was carried for dozens of years on the paper's masthead as October 2. This is a copy of the upper half of the front page of that first edition. The editor was William Doty, "The Kentucky Gentleman." The name comes from the FHC, an eighteenth century student society, known later on campus as The Flat Hat Club. Courtesy of the College Archives*

By 1910 College Corner had an iron fence with a small gateway. The roads were still dirt. The three buildings on the colonial campus attracted little attention from visitors, because all had been modernized. Courtesy of the Colonial Williamsburg Foundation

The 1912 Colonial Echo *provided some interesting glimpses of college life as well as historical vignettes of the school. There were four athletic teams—football, basketball, baseball, and track—and the boxing and wrestling class was a new addition to the physical education/athletic program. Courtesy of the College Archives, College of William and Mary*

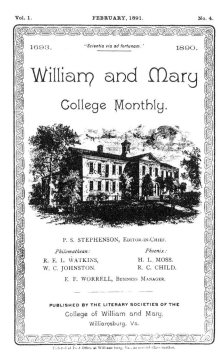

Vol. 1. FEBRUARY, 1891. No. 4.

1693. *"Scientia via ad fortunam."* 1890.

William and Mary

College Monthly.

P. S. STEPHENSON, EDITOR-IN-CHIEF.

Philomathean: *Phoenix:*
R. E. L. WATKINS, H. L. MOSS.
W. C. JOHNSTON. R. C. CHILD.

E. F. WORRELL, BUSINESS MANAGER.

PUBLISHED BY THE LITERARY SOCIETIES OF THE
College of William and Mary,
Williamsburg, Va.

Entered at Post Office at Williamsburg, Va., as second class matter.

This is the front cover of the William and Mary College Monthly, *the first student-run publication at the college. This edition was published in February 1891, as volume four. The first edition was published in 1890. The* College Monthly *was published by the literary societies and was the predecessor to other college literary publications. The* Royalist *and the* Seminar, *student literary efforts, were begun in more recent college years and were published until the fall of 1962, when they merged to form the* William and Mary Review, *the current student literary magazine. Courtesy of the College Archives, College of William and Mary*

113

Tobacco Chewers Club

The Tobacco Chewers Club was very active on campus in 1913-1914. This is the emblem from the yearbook. The officers were: "Sweeney" Blitzer, "Lord High Masticator of the Plug"; George Booth, "chief Desicator of the Sun-cured"; "Yank" Shiers, "boss castigator of scrap," and "Izaak" Walton, "Kate Gravely's affinity." From the 1914 Colonial Echo

The William and Mary baseball team is shown above in action in the spring of 1913 at old Cary Field. This athletic field, which also accommodated football in the fall, was located on the site of the present Bryan Complex. In the distance is the old Bright House, which is now known as Alumni House and located adjacent to the present Cary Field. From the 1913 Colonial Echo; *courtesy of the College Archives, College of William and Mary*

The student council posed for a photograph printed in the 1918 Colonial Echo. *(Unfortunately no one was individually identified and there are nine names and ten men in the photo.) The seniors were Hamilton B. Derieux, president; Clarence Luck Charlton, secretary; Albert P. S. Robinson; and Floyd F. Jenkins. Juniors were Julian A. Brooks and Hinton T. Smith. Sophomores were W. F. C. Ferguson and Chapman S. Moorman; and the freshman was Peter M. Fry, Jr.*

Fraternities have had a long tradition at William and Mary. In 1916 Theta Delta Chi members above were photographed on the front porch of their house. Standing, from left to right, are Cecil Conrad Graves, James Steptoe Robinson, John G. Warburton, Herbert G. Chandler, Albert P. Tobinson, and William M. Brayshaw. Seated, from left to right, are Lewis Perrin Sutherlin; John Morris Presson; George B. Zehrner; Harvey P. Williams, and Thomas Granville Pullen, Jr., Courtesy of the College Archives, College of William and Mary

The William and Mary Choir did not become a major element on campus until after World War II, but in 1917, the Glee Club performed frequently for college occasions. This photograph was taken in the chapel. From the 1917 Colonial Echo

In September 1918, the freshman class posed on the steps of the Sir Christopher Wren Building like all the other classes had posed for years. The year 1918, however, was different; it was the first year women were admitted to William and Mary. From the 1919 Colonial Echo

The newly arrived women at William and Mary had their own Women's Student Council on campus, formed "to represent and to further the best interests of the woman student body." The officers in the 1918-1919 were, from left to right, Margaret Bridges (council member), Catherine Dennis (secretary-treasurer), Martha Barksdale (president), Janet Coleman (vice president), and Ruth Conkey (council member). From the 1919 Colonial Echo

Soon after women arrived on campus, they organized basketball teams. The championship team in 1918-1919 was the Orange Team (top), with members Martha Barksdale, Catherine Dennis, Alice Person, Ruth Harris, Edna Reid and Celeste Ross (captain). The runner-up team was the Black Team, with members Elizabeth Scott (captain), Margaret Thornton, Mary Haile, Margaret Bridges, Janet Coleman, Louise Reid, and Alice Burke. From the 1919 Colonial Echo

Student waiters prepare to serve a meal in the old dining room, circa 1918. Courtesy of the College Archives, College of William and Mary

Women took to the William and Mary stage for the first time in 1918-1919, and in this production they apparently took both the male and female roles in The Three Pills in a Bottle. *Courtesy of the College Archives, College of William and Mary*

The Tyler Hall Club annual photograph in 1918 shows the influence of World War I at the campus. Tyler ceased to be used as a dormitory in the 1980s. Courtesy of the College Archives, College of William and Mary

In December 1918 the Student Army Training Corps (SATC) held a special fire drill outside The Brafferton. Courtesy of the College Archives, College of William and Mary, William Sharp photo

 # To All and Singular

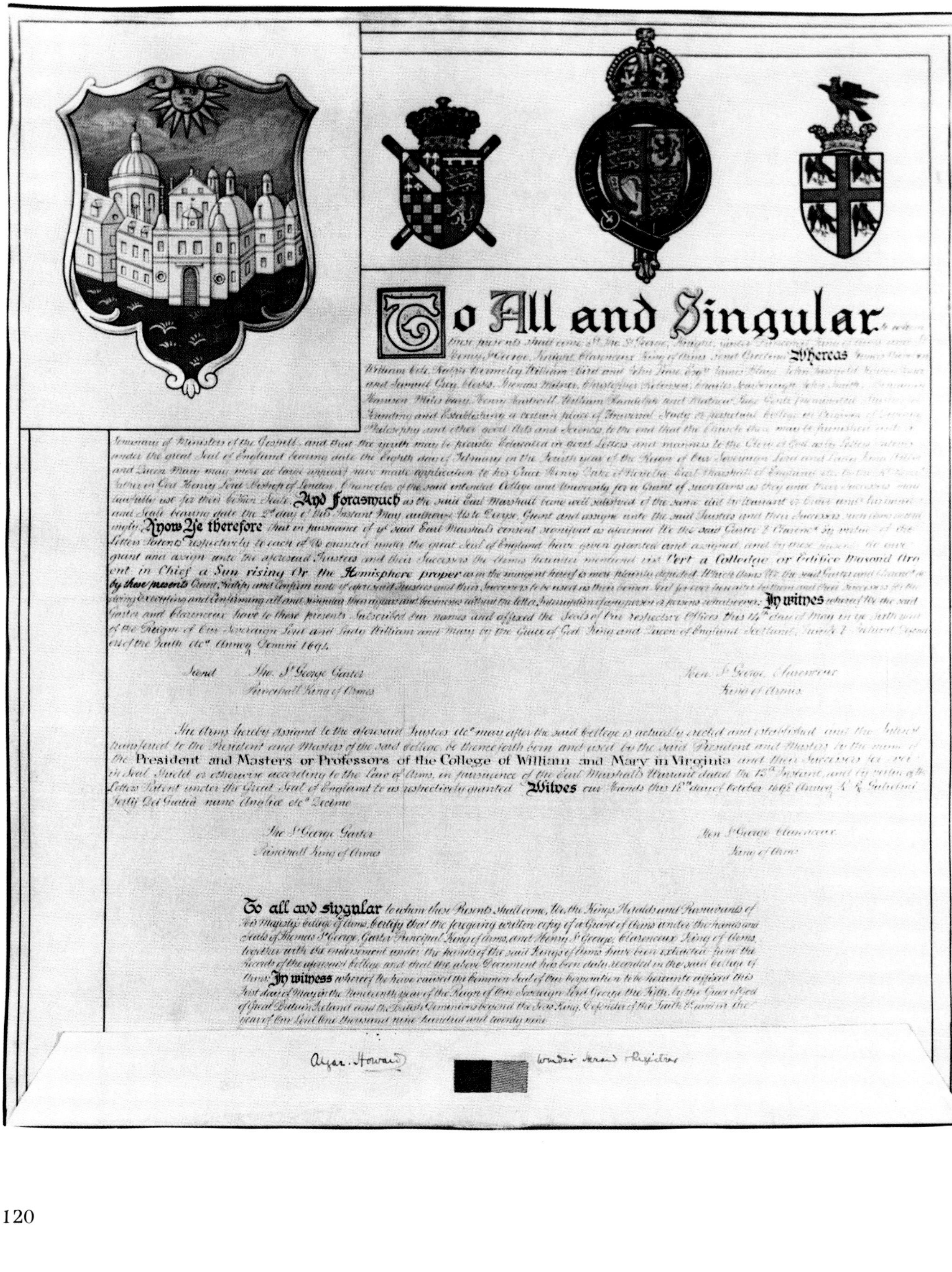

[Text in ornate 17th-century script, largely illegible]

...these presents shall come... Tho. St George, Knight, Garter Principal King of Arms and Henry St George, Knight, Clarenceux King of Arms send Greeting **Whereas**

William Cole, Andrew Wormley, William Bird and John Lane Esq.; James Blair, John Farnifold, Stephen Fouace and Samuel Gray, clerks, Thomas Milner, Christopher Robinson, Charles Scarborough, John Smith, Benjamin Harrison, Miles Cary, Henry Hartwell, William Randolph and Matthew Page Gent. Commonalty have...

...President and Masters or Professors of the College of William and Mary in Virginia and their Successors for ever...

[Signatures]

Tho. St George Garter
Principall King of Arms

Hen. St George Clarenceux
King of Arms

Tho. St George Garter
Principall King of Arms

Hen. St George Clarenceux
King of Arms

To all and singular to whom these Presents shall come, We, the Kings, Heralds and Pursuivants of His Majesty's College of Arms, certify that the foregoing written copy of a Grant of Arms under the hands and Seals of Thomas St George, Garter Principal King of Arms, and Henry St George, Clarenceux King of Arms, together with the endorsement under the hands of the said Kings of Arms have been extracted from the Records of the aforesaid College and that the above Document has been duly recorded in the said College of Arms. In witness whereof we have caused the Common Seal of Our Incorporation to be hereunto affixed this first day of May in the Nineteenth year of the Reign of Our Sovereign Lord George the Fifth, by the Grace of God of Great Britain Ireland and the British Dominions beyond the Sea King, Defender of the Faith &c. and in the year of Our Lord One thousand nine hundred and twenty nine

Algar Howard   Windsor Herald & Registrar

Chapter Ten
1919-1934

Chandler Develops the Modern College

D r. Julian Alvin Carroll Chandler, superintendent of the public schools of the city of Richmond for ten years, was named college president in 1919, after Tyler resigned. His success in securing appropriations from city council doubtless was a major reason for the choice. President Warren G. Harding attended the inauguration program and was awarded an honorary doctor of laws degree.

A professional educator, Chandler immediately set about strengthening the college's programs, which in 1919 were attracting only 131 students. The law school, which had closed in May 1861 because of the Civil War, was reopened in 1920. However, a complete course was not offered until 1922, when the law program became a part of the Marshall-Wythe School of Government and Citizenship, directed for the most part by Dr. John Garland Pollard, who later would become governor. Under the managing editorship of scholar, bibliophile, and long-time librarian Dr. Earl Gregg Swem, a

In April 1929, Dr. J. A. C. Chandler, president, obtained from the College of Arms in London a "certified" copy of the 1694 grant of the coat-of-arms. Until that year, the "Temple" arms, which probably came into use about 1783, were being used. The college arms are in the upper left portion of this modern-day facsimile. Below is the detailed original text which describes the arms. Courtesy of the College Archives, College of William and Mary; Henry Grunder photo

second series of the *William and Mary College Quarterly Historical Magazine* was started.

At the July 1920 board meetings, Chandler proposed that the visitors adopt a plan for the raising of a $1,000,000 endowment fund, which at the time was a staggering sum. Enrollment, however, had more than doubled in one year, to 333 students in 1920, and 400 students were expected for the fall term if accommodations could be found. Actions by Chandler that first year demonstrated to the board that he was not content with William and Mary being a small liberal arts college. Instead, he had in mind a much larger enrollment with expanded programs.

Enrollment for the 1921-1922 session exceeded expectations, rising to 680 students, and Chandler began the building program. Historian and editor Virginius Dabney wrote of Chandler that "his greatest contribution... during his fifteen years as president was in the expansion of the student body and the physical plant... [including an] impressive group of new buildings to add to the venerable colonial structures which had graced the campus since the early eighteenth century." Dabney added that Chandler did not, however, adequately address the improvement of academic standards or the building of a faculty, which he "very probably would have addressed more intensively... if he had lived."

Chandler's building program included: Jefferson Hall (dormitory), 1921; George Preston Blow Gymnasium, 1923; Monroe Hall (dormitory), 1924; Trinkle Hall, the dining hall, 1926; Rogers Hall (science classes), now renamed Chancellor's Hall, 1927; Old Dominion Hall (dormitory), 1927; Barrett Hall (dormitory),

An aerial view shows the William and Mary campus and the city of Williamsburg in June 1920. There were still dirt streets and the campus consisted of just a few buildings. Midway in the photograph are the stands for the first Cary Field (then a baseball diamond) and an adjacent field for athletics. On the right edge (also midway) the ground has been cleared along Jamestown Road for construction of Jefferson Hall, which was completed in 1921. Courtesy of the Office of University Communications, College of William and Mary

named for Dr. Kate Waller Barrett, who contributed substantial funds for its construction, 1927; Washington Hall (classrooms), 1928; Marshall-Wythe (administration), 1935; King Infirmary, now renamed Hunt Hall for Althea Hunt, long-time William and Mary Theatre director, 1930; Brown Hall (dormitory), 1930; Chandler Hall (dormitory), 1931; and Sorority Court (housing), 1920s.

Within weeks of becoming president, Chandler launched an extension program which would be of significant benefit to the college through the years, touching communities and legislators not otherwise directly involved with William and Mary. By 1922, extension classes in Richmond, Norfolk, Newport News, Hampton, and Petersburg had enrolled nearly 680 students. By 1930-1931 the extension classes totaled 1,732.

As an outgrowth of extension programs, in 1925 Chandler established the first successful branch college in the state when the Richmond School of Social Work and Public Health became affiliated with the college. The school later became known as Richmond Professional Institute, which eventually became Virginia Commonwealth University. Property purchased between 1925-1929 by Chandler and Dr. H. H. Hibbs, institute director, included thirty-four major real estate transactions that today form the core campus of the university. In 1930, in response to large attendance in extension division classes in Norfolk, William and Mary opened another division (now Old Dominion University) in that city in September. The two division schools became independent institutions in 1962.

According to Solomon R. Butler and Charles D. Walters in their manuscript, *The Life of Dr. Julian Alvin Carroll Chandler and His Influence on Education in Virginia,* the expansion of the college beyond Williamsburg "encountered opposition from certain people, including some alumni, legislators and even some professors....Some of those who opposed argued that the state already had too many colleges, while some alumni and faculty members insisted that William and Mary should stick to its historic campus and not lower its standards by allowing the name of the institution to be used by those who had never attended the college in Williamsburg. Butler and Walters noted that the opposition continued during the terms of the next two presidents and did not subside until the appointment of Chandler's son as president in 1951. After the Norfolk and Richmond divisions

were separated, William and Mary continued to run its extension programs until they were abandoned in 1972.

Among the key faculty and staff brought to William and Mary during the Chandler years were Dr. K. J. Hoke, dean of the faculty; Dr. E. G. Swem, librarian; Dr. John Garland Pollard, professor of constitutional law; Dr. Donald W. Davis, professor of biology; Richard Lee Morton, professor of history; Dr. W. A. R. Goodwin, professor of biblical literature and religious education; and G. Glenwood Clark, professor of English and journalism; William G. Guy, professor of chemistry; Althea Hunt, director of the William and Mary Theatre; J. Wilfred Lambert, professor of psychology and long-time administrator; Charles F. Marsh, professor of business administration; Grace Warren Landrum, professor of English; Marguerite Wynne-Roberts, assistant professor of physical education and long-time administrator; Albion G. Taylor, professor of economics; A. Pelzer Wagener, professor of ancient languages; and Dudley Warner Woodbridge, professor of law.

Goodwin was the first director of an endowment campaign at William and Mary, and he became involved in a fund-raising program which had a very marked effect on Williamsburg and the college. Goodwin had been rector of Bruton Parish Church from 1903-1909 and had cherished the hope of preserving the still-remaining colonial buildings in the city and in the college yard. He returned to the college in 1923 to direct a $5.7 million endowment campaign, and rekindled his preservation hopes.

In February 1924, Goodwin was in New York City attending a Phi Beta Kappa Society banquet and trying to collect funds for the erection of the first Phi Beta Kappa Memorial Hall at the college. During the program he met philanthropist John D. Rockefeller, Jr., and four months later Goodwin called Rockefeller's office to propose the restoration of the college's three original buildings.

After a two-year wait, Rockefeller finally visited Williamsburg in 1926 with three of his five sons, Laurance, Winthrop, and David; Nelson and John, 3rd, would visit later. By prearrangement Goodwin met Rockefeller on Francis Street and they only discussed the potential college project. Rockefeller asked for time to think about it. On November 27, 1926, Rockefeller returned to Williamsburg to attend the dedication of Phi Beta Kappa Memorial Hall, to which he had made a significant contribution. Rockefeller told Goodwin

The women's physical training class is shown in the winter of 1920-1921. It is believed the class was conducted on the lawn by Richmond Road. Courtesy of the College Archives, College of William and Mary

he was interested in the plan and asked him to have drawings prepared of the three college buildings and a general layout of the town.

Soon after his visit, Goodwin wrote Rockefeller that several eighteenth-century homes in the town were available for purchase; on December 7, 1926, Rockefeller wired Goodwin to buy the Ludwell-Paradise House and signed the telegram, "David's Father." Thus, the Williamsburg restoration was born.

In 1927, discussion of the details of the college project began. Chandler wanted two colonial-style pavilions constructed to the rear, on either side of the main building, to compensate for classrooms that would be lost when the main building was restored. Although the architects realized that such buildings did not exist in the eighteenth century, the concept was a way of giving the college much-needed classroom space. The restoration project for the main building was first designed with a "Memorial Hall" stretching along the front. Later, Rockefeller decided to restore only what was original to the eighteenth century. Therefore, the college accepted $400,000 to restore the main building, and the proposed $100,000 for the pavilions was used to restore The Brafferton and the President's House. The restoration work was accomplished at Rockefeller's direction, encouraging him to invest countless millions of dollars in the restoration and reconstruction of colonial Williamsburg.

The main building, which is now called the Sir Christopher Wren Building, was under reconstruction from 1928-1931. (In 1968, several rooms in the building were restored and fitted with appropriate colonial furniture by the Colonial Williamsburg Foundation and were opened to the public by the college.) The President's House exterior restoration was accomplished from April to September, 1931, while The Brafferton was restored from December 1931 to June 1932.

Chandler did not hesitate to endorse, and at times actively support, certain candidates for political office and even "engaged in politics, but his main motive seems to have been the enhancement of the cause of education especially the kind that pertained to the College of William and Mary," Butler and Walters wrote. "Some have claimed that Chandler could have succeeded Governor Harry F. Byrd," but he declined, which probably had much to do with the eventual selection of Dr. Pollard as a candidate in 1929.

In October 1931, college officials participated in the sesquicentennial of the Battle of Yorktown, and on October 19 the faculty and administration traveled to the battlefield program to present an honorary doctor of laws degree to President Herbert C. Hoover, who was attending the festivities.

By the spring of 1934, Chandler was seriously ill. He died in a Norfolk hospital on May 31, 1934.

Just prior to his death, in February, state auditor L. McCarthy Downs issued a report critical of the way various accounts had been handled at the college. There was never any intimation that money had been used fraudulently, but it was known that Chandler had routinely transferred money from account to account covering expenses.

Newspaper accounts of the report were highly overblown. Although Chandler was too ill to respond personally, the board of visitors wrote a lengthy reply to Governor George C. Perry. In the end, the college had to pay a small amount owed to the state, but Downs, after reviewing the college records, agreed with a major board contention that college endowment money had been spent to construct many of the buildings.

Vernon M. Nunn, long-time treasurer of the college, explained that as an outgrowth of the Downs report state auditors agreed to allow the college to restore $548,000 to the endowment through student dormitory receipts. "It never occurred to Dr. Chandler to do anything wrong. William and Mary was his life. He had foresight and I do not believe the college has yet achieved the potential he dreamed about. He was really the father of modern William and Mary." Thus, through added endowment money, Chandler's work, even after his death, proved the impetus for the current William and Mary Endowment Association program.

This is a photograph of the freshman class in clothing construction in the home economics department, circa 1920-1922. Courtesy of the College Archives, College of William and Mary

In September 1920, just two years after women were first admitted to William and Mary, sororities began to develop. Delta Phi Kappa sorority, a local, was founded at the college. Its colors were purple and white and the flower was the violet. The charter members were: Hilda Butler, Ruth Cashion, Sarah Cuthrell, Helen Featherstone, Inez Grey, Etta Henderson, Sallie Mapp Jacob, Cecil Norfleet, Alice Person, Dorothy Reeve, Sara Rhoades, and Mavis Taylor. About the same time other locals, Delta Phi Kappa and Upsilon Delta Beta, also were founded at the college. The locals gave way to national sororities and in 1922 Chi Omega was the first national sorority established on campus. In September 1925, Delta Phi Kappa became Pi Beta Phi. From the 1921 Colonial Echo

This is believed to be a photograph of what has been called Boundary Street Dormitory II. Used for a time in the early 1920s as a hardware store, the building was rented by the college between 1923 and 1926 and used as a men's dormitory. Courtesy of the College Archives, College of William and Mary

The 1921 baseball team was photographed for the Colonial Echo. Second from right, second row, is coach James D. Driver, who was coach and athletic director for four years. He later served as athletic director at the University of Virginia (for eight years) and at the University of South Carolina. A William and Mary alumnus, he was captain of the football, baseball, basketball, and track teams in his senior year. From the 1921 Colonial Echo

Dr. J. A. C. Chandler was inaugurated president of William and Mary on October 19, 1921 in ceremonies attended by Warren Harding, president of the United States. Harding is shown here receiving an honorary doctor of laws degree from college rector John Hardy Dillard. Dr. Chandler is at the far right. From the 1922 Colonial Echo

Dr. J. A. C. Chandler (far right), college president, was the architect for the main campus and the Reverend W. A. R. Goodwin (second from the right) was hired in 1923 as a professor and fund raiser. Goodwin succeeded in securing money for many of the academic buildings and residences that were added to the old campus. Courtesy of the College Archives, College of William and Mary

Spectators gather around the movie filming of D. W. Griffith's America outside The Brafferton on November 17, 1923. The mules and wagon (left) were props for the filming. Courtesy of the Society of the Alumni; Herbert L. Ganter photo

128

In 1923 a musical group called The Indian Serenaders, was formed by J. C. Phillips (1924) and began playing at the Saturday night campus dances and at the Pocahontas Tea Room near campus. The group performed on radio for the first time in 1925-1926 on WRVA in Richmond. The Indian Serenaders made a "triumphal tour" of Europe, also in 1926, and continued as an organization until 1928. Other student bands were formed in the 1930s, but none attracted the attention of the earlier Serenaders. In this 1926 picture, E. Cotton Rawls, cornet player and group manager, is standing in the rear with an unidentified trombone player. In front, from left to right, are Townley Gamble, saxophone; J. M. "Buck" Weaver, banjo; Harry Blair, traps; Robert Pully, piano; and H. C. Westcott, saxophone. Courtesy of the Society of the Alumni

On May 25, 1924, the Knights of Columbus held the first annual field mass in the courtyard of the Sir Christopher Wren Building. Notice the great hall wing of the building (in the rear) had been renovated and a second floor built into the large room. An exterior door also was put into the wall. Courtesy of the College Archives, College of William and Mary

The brothers of Kappa Alpha fraternity pose for their annual photograph in 1924-1925 on the front steps of their house, known for many years as Bright House after the farm that had stood on the site. After World War II, the house was divided into apartments and rented to faculty and in 1972 was renovated and became the Alumni House. Courtesy of the College Archives, College of William and Mary

For many years, the annual alumni gathering at William and Mary was held to coincide with commencement. These are some of the alumni who attended the June 10, 1924 alumni dinner. College President Dr. J. A. C. Chandler is in the light suit, front row, in the middle of the walk. Notice the dresses and suits of the roaring twenties. Courtesy of the College Archives, College of William and Mary

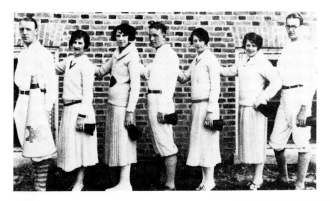

The 1924-1925 cheerleaders led cheers for the "Fighting Indians" as the athletic teams were called. The school colors then were orange and black, having been changed from orange and white at the turn of the century. And the school yell also had been modernized from the 1899 yell, which was William and Mary, Vir-gin-i-a, Croatan, Powhatan, Ha! Ha! Ha! *From the 1925* Colonial Echo

This view of the front campus from College Corner and the Duke of Gloucester Street is circa 1925 and is prior to the restoration of the Sir Christopher Wren Building to its colonial appearance. Note the street had been surfaced and cement front steps had been erected at the campus entrance. *Courtesy of the Colonial Williamsburg Foundation*

On June 3, 1925, formal Masonic rites were held in conjunction with the cornerstone laying of old Phi Beta Kappa Hall. *Courtesy of the College Archives, College of William and Mary*

By 1926 the college had further expanded across Jamestown Road. From left to right, the buildings fronting the road and main campus were Tyler Hall, the Deanery (with the irregular roof and porch, for several years the house of Kappa Kappa Gamma sorority), Ewell Hall (the old college hotel with the large porch), and Taliaferro Hall. At the far right is The Brafferton on the colonial campus. Courtesy of the Colonial Williamsburg Foundation

The sesquicentennial celebration of the Virginia Declaration for Independence was held at the college on May 15, 1926. This aerial view shows the crowd gathered behind the Sir Christopher Wren Building for the public program. Notice that the library had been enlarged (lower left) and Phi Beta Kappa Memorial Hall was nearing completion (at right). Courtesy of the College Archives, College of William and Mary

This is a portion of the business district along Duke of Gloucester Street near College Corner about 1925. The cement street had been laid and the island with its telephone poles had been put in the middle. The Sir Christopher Wren Building and the college campus are at the end of the street. Courtesy of the Richmond Times-Dispatch

United States President Calvin Coolidge attended the sesquicentennial anniversary of the Virginia Declaration for Independence on May 15, 1926. He addressed the crowd from beneath a large tent erected in the courtyard of the Sir Christopher Wren Building. Coolidge is shown with the governor of Virginia, Harry F. Byrd, after they received honorary degrees; the men are carrying their degree citations. College rector John Hardy Dillard is behind Byrd. Courtesy of the College Archives, College of William and Mary

Taken looking toward town from the campus, circa 1925, this photograph shows the new concrete pavement with the grass plot down the middle. The spire of Bruton Parish Church can be seen in the center background. Courtesy of the Richmond Times-Dispatch

On December 4, 1926 the William and Mary football team traveled to Chattanooga, Tennessee for its first post-season game. According to the 1927 Colonial Echo, the "Fighting Virginians" as the team also was called, defeated Chattanooga, 9-6, "thereby establishing a good claim to the Southern title," even though for the season the team had a 5-4 record. This team photograph was taken on top of Lookout Mountain; the team captain was Arthur Matsu and the football coach and director of athletics was J. Wilder Tasker. Courtesy of the Men's Athletic Association, College of William and Mary

The first night football in the East was played on September 24, 1927 under the new lights at Cary Field. At that time it was the largest crowd ever to witness a William and Mary football game according to newspaper accounts. Unfortunately, Catholic University won, 12-0. The photograph shows the lights and the freshmen huddling on the field prior to the game. From the 1928 Colonial Echo

Work had just begun on the Sir Christopher Wren Building in this early 1928 photograph. Note that the great hall wing had been divided and a second floor added. The great round windows and rear doorway had been bricked shut. In the left foreground is the college sundial, a gift of the first staff of The Flat Hat, the student newspaper founded on October 3, 1911. Courtesy of the Colonial Williamsburg Foundation

The Sir Christopher Wren Building was in shabby condition when restoration work began in late 1927. This photograph shows a classroom with an electric light bulb hanging from the ceiling and a large stove in the rear. Courtesy of the Colonial Williamsburg Foundation

The massive walls of the second version of the Sir Christopher Wren Building, its great hall, and the chapel wing that was added later are the only portions of the building which survived the 1859 fire, and they only survived up to the top of the second story windows. Courtesy of the Colonial Williamsburg Foundation

During the restoration, the interior of the Sir Christopher Wren Building was gutted. This is a view of the chapel wing with the flooring removed and the crypts underneath exposed. Several colonial personages were buried under the chapel floor, including Peyton Randolph, first president of the Continental Congress and Lord Botetourt, whose crypt is believed to be one of the two in the left foreground. Courtesy of the Colonial Williamsburg Foundation

The college chapel was very Victorian in appearance before the Sir Christopher Wren Building was restored through the auspices of John D. Rockefeller, Jr's. restoration organization. The three portraits on the rear wall are (from left) Benjamin S. Ewell (college president), James Blair (first college president), and Mrs. Blair (Sarah Harrison Blair). Courtesy of the Colonial Williamsburg Foundation

In January 1931, most of the exterior restoration work had been completed on the Sir Christopher Wren Building. Notice that on the great hall wing (left) the dark brick denotes the roof line of the old building. Courtesy of the Colonial Williamsburg Foundation

137

The first homecoming parade was held in 1929, and from then until 1982 its route was from the campus down Duke of Gloucester Street to the capitol building and then back up the street. Beginning in 1982, the parade formed at the capitol and came along the street just once. This was the first float in the 1929 parade. It depicted the Reverend James Blair receiving the college charter from King William III and Queen Mary II. Courtesy of the College Archives, College of William and Mary; Howard Scammon photo

On March 15, 1930 a major fire struck old Rogers Hall (now Chancellors Hall). These photographs show the fire burning the roof and the third floor of the building. The total damage was $70,142 (in Depression-era dollars). Courtesy of Dr. Davis Y. Paschall

Before the restoration of the Sir Christopher Wren Building, between 1927 and 1931, these round windows at the rear of the great hall had been bricked closed because a second floor was placed in the room to create more classroom space in the building. With the restoration, however, the attractive windows were restored and the second floor removed. The brickwork around the doorway and windows is original to the colonial building. Courtesy of the Office of University Communications, College of William and Mary

As decreed by the royal charter, William and Mary is required to pay its quitrents annually with two Latin verses. On November 5, 1930 the payment was delivered to Governor John Garland Pollard (center), former college professor of government and citizenship. From left to right are William Leary Scott; Dr. A. Pelzer Wagener, professor of ancient languages; Dr. J. A. C. Chandler, college president; Pollard; Dr. Earl Gregg Swem, librarian, with the college mace; Dr. Kremer J. Hoke, dean of the college; Joseph Wayne Shoemaker; and Col. John W. Williams, clerk of the house of delegates. Courtesy of the College Archives, College of William and Mary

In 1931 hangars were built at the college airport when the flight school was begun at William and Mary. Y. O. Kent (1930) and Julian Chandler, son of Dr. J. A. C. Chandler, were two of the first four students. The aeronautics program was the first, and ultimately one of the best, of any college in the nation. The program director was Colonel E. C. Popp, and Kent and young Chandler later became instructors. Courtesy of the College Archives, College of William and Mary

The 1740 Bodleian plate shown in Chapter Five was discovered in December 1939 at the Bodleian Library at Oxford University. It contained a rear view of the Sir Christopher Wren Building which showed that the rear elevation of the building had three complete bricked floors and three hipped roofs. This discovery caused architects to completely redraw the restoration plans for the building and delayed its completion by several months as steel beams, already in place, had to be cut out and refitted.Courtesy of the Colonial Williamsburg Foundation

In 1930-1931, the old Citizenship Building was nearing its final year. It stood between the Sir Christopher Wren Building and old Phi Beta Kappa Hall (at the rear of the photograph). It was destroyed after restoration of the Wren Building was completed. Courtesy of the Colonial Williamsburg Foundation; Virginia Brown Smith photo

In the 1920s and 1930s May Day celebrations were an important event on campus and attracted much community attention. This is a May Day program in 1931 on the front campus. Courtesy of the College Archives, College of William and Mary

The second Ewell Hall, the science building, stood on campus between the President's House and the old college library. It was torn down in 1931 after the restoration of the Wren Building. This photograph during the 1930-1931 school term shows students going to and from classes. The library is at the far left and part of the great hall is at right. Courtesy of the Colonial Williamsburg Foundation; Virginia Brown Smith photo

In the 1930-1931 season, the William and Mary Players (later the William and Mary Theatre), saw the accomplishment of the spectacular "Vergilian Pageant" performed outdoors at night in the Players Dell. The Players' first production was in 1926 when Professor Althea Hunt directed The Goose Hangs High, the play that formally opened old Phi Beta Kappa Hall as a theatre. In 1928 the tradition of an annual Shakespearean production was begun with The Taming of the Shrew. Courtesy of the College Archives, College of William and Mary

On October 18, 1931, General of the Armies John J. Pershing spoke at William and Mary at the program to dedicate the memorial tablet at the Sir Christopher Wren Building. The tablet honors French soldiers who died in Williamsburg during and after the 1781 Yorktown campaign. *Courtesy of the Colonial Williamsburg Foundation*

On October 19, 1931, for the sesquicentennial of the surrender at Yorktown, the faculty of the college journeyed to the celebration in Yorktown to present an honorary doctor of laws degree to United States President Herbert C. Hoover. It is believed to have been the only degree ever presented away from the campus. Rector James Hardy Dillard (left) and Dr. J. A. C. Chandler, college president (right), are shown with Hoover, who has his degree in hand. The presentation took place in a tent. *Courtesy of the National Park Service;* Richmond Times-Dispatch *photo*

143

The Brafferton and the President's House were restored through the generosity of John D. Rockefeller, Jr., after the Sir Christopher Wren building had been restored. This photograph, taken January 4, 1932, shows work on The Brafferton after the roof and much of the interior had been removed. Courtesy of the Colonial Williamsburg Foundation

A view of the colonial campus around 1933 shows the Sir Christopher Wren Building (middle), The Brafferton (left), and the President's House (right). Many tall trees still lined the main walks. Courtesy of the Colonial Williamsburg Foundation

The Sir Christopher Wren Building was rededicated on September 16, 1931, following its restoration. Rector John Hardy Dillard (in academic garb) receives the key to the building from W. S. Perry, principal architect of the project. Dr. Earl Gregg Swem, college librarian, is carrying the college mace, and just above him is John Stewart Bryan, the member of the board of visitors who would become the next college president. Althea Hunt, director of the William and Mary Theatre, is in the front row, far left, and to the right of Swem are faculty members Alma Wilkin, Martha Barksdale, and L. Tucker Jones (front right). Courtesy of the Colonial Williamsburg Foundation

The William and Mary players, directed by Althea Hunt, performed a special pageant at Jamestown Island on May 13, 1932 to commemorate the 325th anniversary of the founding of the Jamestown settlement. This scene is the marriage of Pocahontas. Courtesy of the College Archives, College of William and Mary; Howard Scammon photo

This 1932 picture of the rear of the Sir Christopher Wren Building shows its restoration. The Sunken Garden had not yet been constructed, though small magnolia trees had been planted around what would be the garden's edge. Courtesy of the Colonial Williamsburg Foundation

Chapter Eleven
1934-1960

"Camelot," Academics, and the Ship of State

The board of visitors did not have to look far in its search for a successor to Dr. J. A. C. Chandler. From 1926 to 1934, the board's vice rector was John Stewart Bryan of Richmond, a wealthy newspaper publisher who succeeded to the presidency as the Great Depression was ending. Maintaining his position as publisher of *The Richmond News Leader,* and later the *Times-Dispatch,* which he repurchased in 1940, Bryan divided his time between Richmond and Williamsburg. He had received B.A. and M.A. degrees from the University of Virginia and a bachelor of law degree from Harvard University.

Early in his career, he sought to strengthen the liberal arts at the college, specifically history, English, and philosophy, with the appointments between 1934 and 1937 of a number of professors who were to be known later in William and Mary lore as the Harvard University group: Dr. Murray Eugene Borish (English); Dr. Harold Lees Fowler (history); Dr. James W. Miller (philosophy); Dr. Francis H. Haserot (philosophy); Dr. Charles Harrison (English); Dr. Lionel Laing (government); Dr. William R. Richardson (English); and Frederick W. Hoeing (history) joined prominent Harvard graduates already on campus, Dr. Donald Davis (biology); Dr. Jess Jackson (English); Dr. Archie G. Ryland (French), and Dr. Raymond L. Taylor (biology). By 1937, Bryan had been elected to the Harvard board of overseers.

Dean of the Faculty E. Gordon Bell of Dartmouth College became a confidant of Bryan, recommending potential faculty members and helping him determine what kind of liberal arts model would be best suited for William and Mary.

William and Mary had made history in 1779 when, during the Jeffersonian reorganization, Professor Robert Andrews introduced the study of the fine arts into his professorship of moral philosophy. It was the first such academic presentation in American college history. Unfortunately, the fine arts aspect did not survive long and fine arts at William and Mary did not see a renaissance until 1935, when Bryan hired Yale University architecture graduate Leslie Cheek, Jr., to teach courses on the history of architecture.

The success of the courses led Cheek to propose to Bryan the development of an entire undergraduate department of fine arts, offering the history of painting, sculpture, and architecture, as well as music and theatre. Under Cheek the department flourished; Miss Althea Hunt, hired during the Chandler administration, continued to nurture the growing theatre program. Old Taliaferro Hall on Jamestown Road was completely refurbished for the

The 1939 Christmas party in old Phi Beta Kappa Memorial Hall was a gala event. President Bryan (center) is shown in his double-bottom wig and colonial attire as lord of the manor. The woman on his arm is Mrs. Douglas Southall Freeman. L. Tucker Jones (right), in colonial military uniform, acted as the marshal for such occasions. Courtesy of the Colonial Williamsburg Foundation

On October 20, 1934, John Stewart
Bryan was inaugurated as president
of William and Mary in a program
held on the rear portico of the Sir
Christopher Wren Building. United
States President Franklin D. Roose-
velt spoke and received an honorary
doctor of laws degree. Rector John
Hardy Dillard is seated at the right of
this picture. Courtesy of the Richmond Times-Dispatch; Colonial
Williamsburg Foundation photo

An aerial view shows the college
campus in the spring of 1934.
Construction had just begun on the
football stadium shown at the bottom
of the photograph and the Sunken
Garden had not yet been dug. However, the main campus was complete,
with the exception of Landrum Hall,
opened in 1959. Courtesy of the
Office of University Communications,
College of William and Mary

In the spring of 1935, there was just a field in the middle of campus, with academic buildings on either side. Rogers Hall (now Chancellors Hall) and the old library (now St. George Tucker Hall) were on the left, and old Phi Beta Kappa Hall (now Ewell Hall) and Washington Hall were on the right. Courtesy of the College Archives, College of William and Mary

This photograph was taken in the fall of 1935. The stadium at Cary Field had not been finished, and the colonnade at the north end was still under construction. The residential area northwest of campus was just beginning to be developed and College Terrace, with its divided road, can be seen in the upper left of the photograph. Courtesy of the Richmond Times-Dispatch

fine arts program. (The old building had a decorative fountain with live fish in a pool.)

In 1939 there was a move by Bryan and the visitors to end the law program, which had only been reestablished in 1922. Since that time only twenty-three degrees had been granted and there were only fifty-two students enrolled, few of them seeking law degrees. On May 29, 1939, the visitors, supported by Bryan, voted 5-2 to end the degree granting program and the professional courses in June 1940, but to continue law courses which would be of a more cultural, college-wide interest.

Within days, alumni, friends, and students learned of the board's decision and strongly lobbied for the law school's retention. Only after an outpouring of concern and pledges from alumni of financial support did Bryan and the board on June 2, decide to reverse their positions; the visitors voted 8-1 to continue the law school.

Bryan was extremely popular with the students and faculty, and Dr. James W. Miller later reminisced, "Mr. Bryan made everybody in the faculty feel at home at William and Mary and not threatened as they may have felt under the Chandler Administration." Black-tie dress was *de rigueur* for evening entertainments and the social life of the campus was active during the Bryan years. Several professors on campus described this period as "Camelot," reflecting the president's accent on the "good life," still amid some poor economic times. Even the students enjoyed gala festivities, such as the annual Christmas party and the June Finals Ball given by the president, largely at his expense.

The Christmas party was held in the auditorium of old Phi Beta Kappa Hall, with Bryan presiding in his colonial attire as lord of the manor, complete with double-bottom wig. He sat enthroned on stage with the faculty and staff also in appropriate colonial costumes. Various student organizations presented skits and performances.

The Sunken Garden, designed by landscape architect Charles Gillette in a fashion reminiscent of the grounds of London's Chelsea Hospital, was completed in 1935 and became the scene for the June Finals Ball, under the stars. A dance floor was constructed with adjacent orchestra platform and giant urns of flowers were situated throughout the area. During this era the famous nationally-known dance bands of Hal Kemp, Gene Krupa, Sammy Kaye, Woody Herman, Johnny Long, and Glenn Miller played at William and Mary.

In 1942, Bryan announced his resignation

This picture shows the board of managers of the Society of the Alumni of the College of William and Mary in the fall of 1936. From left to right are Robert Perry Wallace, secretary-treasurer; Charles P. McCurdy, Jr., who later would become executive-secretary; Charles A. Taylor, Jr., executive secretary; Sidney B. Hall; Joseph E. Healy, president; A. Ralph Koontz; James Malcolm Bridges; and Cornelia Storrs Adair (for whom the women's gymnasium was named in 1965). Courtesy of the Office of University Communications, College of William and Mary

In June 1934, the Finals Dance was held for the first time in the new Sunken Garden. A dance floor was set up on the grass near the Wren Building end. There were elaborate decorations, including a giant urn, filled with magnolias, in the middle of the dance floor. Frank Lamarr and his orchestra provided the music. Other famous dance bands to perform in succeeding years were the Hal Kemp, Glenn Miller, and Woody Herman bands. The pomp and splendor of this dance, as well as the annual Christmas Party, were financed primarily by College President John Stewart Bryan. From the 1937 Colonial Echo

During the winter of 1935-1936, the boxwood hedge was planted around the edge of the Sunken Garden. The hedge, then only two-and-a-half feet high, has now grown to a height of about twelve feet or more. The Sir Christopher Wren Building is at the far left, with old Phi Beta Kappa Hall (now Ewell Hall) and Washington Hall at the far right. The garden has been used for numerous events, including formal dances and parties under tents. For many years the United States Army Reserve Officer Training Corps (ROTC) used it for weekly drills, and students have routinely studied there, played touch football and soccer, and even tossed frisbees. Courtesy of the Office of University Communications, College of William and Mary

The boat house at Lake Matoaka, near the present Common Glory amphitheatre, was built in 1935 by the Civilian Conservation Corps and the National Park Service as part of Matoaka Park. The National Park Service gave the park to the college. It included about 1,200 acres of land, on which there were picnic shelters and a system of bridle paths. This photograph was taken about 1939. Courtesy of the Office of University Communications, College of William and Mary

The bridle paths of Matoaka Park skirted the edge of the lake at several spots. College students on horseback and in canoes enjoy the park in this photograph, circa 1937. Courtesy of the Office of University Communications, College of William and Mary

On November 17, 1934, the Society of the Alumni recognized twenty-four recipients of the newly established Alumni Medallion for service and loyalty. The medallion, given annually, is the highest honor that the society can bestow on an alumnus. Courtesy of the Society of the Alumni

Homecoming 1938 was the golden reunion for men who had entered William and Mary in 1888 when the college reopened after the silent years. The reunion members posed around classmate Herbert Lee Bridges, who was confined to a wheelchair. From left to right were: Dr. R. W. Sturgis, Granville W. Gary, T. Cecil Clopton, Rosser Lee Marston, Percy S. Stephenson, Gratz Ross Minton, W. W. Allmond, Benjamin Lewis Carter, George Walter Mapp, Fernando S. Farrar (at rear), Russell Lynn, J. W. Stockley, H. Pitts, Richard H. White, George Preston Coleman, William Carter Stubbs and William Churchill Lyons Taliaferro. Courtesy of the Office of University Communications, College of William and Mary

This cabin at Squirrel Point in Matoaka Park was a popular retreat for students and faculty, who held parties there. This photograph is circa 1937. Courtesy of the College Archives, College of William and Mary

John Peyton Little, Jr., (right) then the second oldest living alumnus of the college, rode in the 1937 homecoming parade with President John Stewart Bryan. Bryan brought the horse-drawn carriage to Williamsburg from his Richmond home, Laburnum. The carriage remained in town until about 1970, and was used by the Kappa Alpha fraternity for several of their "Old South" celebrations. Courtesy of the Richmond Times-Dispatch

On May 7, 1938, nationally-known artist Georgia O'Keeffe was presented by William and Mary with an honorary doctor of fine arts degree. Miss O'Keeffe, a former Williamsburg resident, also was recognized by having a major exhibition of her work—the first showing of her paintings anywhere in the South. In conjunction with O'Keeffe's campus visit and exhibition, Mrs. John D. Rockefeller, Jr., gave the college a picture by the artist, painted in 1932. It is a white flower, painted in oil on a plywood panel. Courtesy of the College Art Collection, College of William and Mary; Copyright Georgia O'Keeffe

153

The 1939 Christmas party and dance in old Phi Beta Kappa Hall was attended by most of the students and faculty, and special invited guests. Here some of the guests prepare to dance. From right to left are Channing Hall, a member of the board of visitors; unidentified; Amadeo Obici, a member of the board of visitors; and Dudley W. Woodbridge, professor of law. The last two men in the line are unidentified. Courtesy of the Colonial Williamsburg Foundation

The Christmas party tradition at the college was established in 1934 by President John Stewart Bryan. The festivities were traditionally held in the auditorium of old Phi Beta Kappa Hall. All the seats were taken out and the sororities and fraternities performed skits. The faculty wore colonial costumes and the students also wore various costumes. From the 1940 Colonial Echo

Another important celebration on campus in the late 1930s was the bringing in of the yule log. Here costumed students bring in the boar's head prior to the log being brought into the great hall. The tradition of the yule log ceremony is still part of the annual holiday activities on campus. Courtesy of the Colonial Williamsburg Foundation

By the mid-1930s, homecoming had also become an important event on the annual college calendar. L. Tucker Jones, professor of physical education, was the parade marshal for all the parades from 1929 until 1941, when World War II disrupted campus life. In this 1920s picture, notice that the floats were still drawn by horses and mules and the automobiles were gaily decorated. *Courtesy of the Colonial Williamsburg Foundation*

Phi Kappa Tau fraternity won third prize in the November 18, 1939 homecoming parade; few people remember who won first. *Courtesy of the College Archives, College of William and Mary*

Throughout the 1930s the Players Dell in Matoaka Park attracted actors who performed outdoors. The dell is believed to have been not far from where the old Founders Theatre is located to the west of Adair Gymnasium. Courtesy of the Colonial Williamsburg Foundation

"An evening in a men's dormitory" is the caption of this photograph in a William and Mary catalogue published in April 1940. It is the lounge in Monroe Hall, which until the late 1970s was a men's dormitory and is now a women's residence hall. Courtesy of the College of William and Mary

In 1939, as part of the continuing interest in the expansion of the fine arts at William and Mary, John Stewart Bryan presented the school a painting by John Singleton Copley, The Battle of Dunkirk. *For many years the painting hung in Trinkle Hall over the large mantle. Courtesy of the College Art Collection, College of William and Mary*

The winter of 1940 was cold, and ice covered Lake Matoaka for many weeks. Students, faculty, and townspeople spent many afternoons ice skating on the lake. Pictured from left to right are Donald Meiklejohn, associate professor of philosophy; Marguerite Wynne-Roberts, assistant dean of women; Gladys Guy; and Dr. William G. Guy, professor of chemistry. Courtesy of Frances Robb

Carl Voyles (right) and Ruben McCray compiled the best back-to-back coaching record in the history of William and Mary football. Voyles, called the "Silver Tongue" because of his way with words, compiled the best winning percentage in his four years, winning twenty-nine, losing seven, and tying three games between 1939 and 1942. The 1942 team coached by Voyles compiled the second best season (9-1-1) in the school's history. McCray, his assistant, became head coach in 1944. (World War II eliminated the 1943 season.) During his seven seasons, which ended in 1950, McCray won forty-two games, lost twenty-one, and tied three. From the 1943 Colonial Echo

Beginning in 1937, the William and Mary mascot was Wampo, an Indian pony which appeared at most of the college home football games for several years. Tim Hanson and Jimmy Keillor rode tandem bareback in full Indian attire to celebrate each score. In this picture from a college catalogue published in April 1940, Sterling Strange is on Wampo. Courtesy of the College of William and Mary

The 1942 William and Mary football team won the Southern Conference Championship, winning nine games. The 14-7 record for the season included a victory over the University of Oklahoma, a tie with the United States Naval Academy, and a loss to the powerful North Carolina Preflight. From left to right are: Front row—Hubard, Johnson, Korczowski, Knox, Warrington, Bass, Vandeweghe, Ramsey, Fields, Holloway, Clowes, and Forkovitch. Second row—Weaver, Sazio, Chipok, Blagg, Safko, H. Knox, Poplinger, Johns, Kline, Wright, and Irvin. Back Row—Steckroth, Ream, Schultz, Graham, Brown, Abbotts, Bucher, Longacre, Grimbowitz, Gooden, and Freeman. The captain of the team was Marvin Bass, who coached the 1951 William and Mary football team and later became a professional football coach. Courtesy of the Men's Athletic Association, College of William and Mary

In 1943 the most attractive entrance to the college was off Richmond Road at what has become known as the Ewell gateway, an imposing structure of brick and iron erected as a memorial to former college President Benjamin Stoddert Ewell. Note the twin statues of King William III (left) and Queen Mary II on the pillars. The gate itself was removed about a decade later, but the gateway remains with its statues. Courtesy of the Richmond Times-Dispatch

and the board named him chancellor of the college, the first to hold the post since historian Hugh Blair Grigsby served from 1871 to 1881. Bryan died in Richmond in 1944.

The visitors wasted little time in naming Dr. John Edwin Pomfret, dean of the senior college and graduate school at Vanderbilt University, as the new president. A strong educator and keen scholar, Pomfret never had a chance to put his own ideas and concepts to work before World War II stripped William and Mary, like most other colleges, of its male students. His task was a very complex one: preserving the college.

On February 22, 1943, the United States Naval Training School for Chaplains opened at the college, utilizing much of the Marshall-Wythe Hall for its operations. Dean J. Wilfred Lambert, who had joined the navy earlier, was assigned to the school and served as liaison with the college. The chaplain school ended in 1945.

In December 1943, the Institute of Early American History and Culture was formed, and in January 1944 the *William and Mary Quarterly* began its third series as a "magazine of early American history, institutions, and culture," under the editorship of Dr. Richard Lee Morton, professor of history. United States President Harry S Truman visited the school on October 11, 1948, for Canadian-American Day, and, continuing a college tradition, received an honorary doctor of laws degree.

William and Mary's only major men's national athletic team championships came in 1947 and 1948 when tennis, long popular at the school, hit the sports pages. By any standard, from 1946 through 1950, William and Mary's tennis dynasty, under Dr. Sharvey Umbeck, a sociology professor, was one of the greatest in college sports history. The team had three perfect seasons and a five-year, eighty-two-match winning streak, then an NCAA record. Garner Larned won the NCAA singles title in 1947 and Bernard "Tut" Bartzen and Fred Kovaleski teamed to win the NCAA doubles championship in 1948.

During the last years of the Bryan administration, beginning in 1939 and into the Pomfret years, football became increasingly important on the campus, and at least until 1950 it was considered "big-time," with the Indians going to two bowl games and achieving the best winning record in the school's history.

The pressure was there to keep winning. But the "golden era" was to end when college officials determined that high school transcripts of football players applying for admission were being altered. There also were cases of students in college getting credit for courses they did not attend. Unfortunately for Pomfret, at the outset of the allegations he could not believe that certain coaches whom he had trusted and supported could betray the college in this manner. The athletic controversy resulted in the resignation of a number of the coaches, while the faculty urged a major reduction in intercollegiate athletics, especially football.

On September 17, 1951, the college's faculty unanimously adopted a statement concerning the athletic controversy. The statement said: "We are agreed that the fundamental cause is an athletic policy which at William and Mary, as at many other American colleges and universities, has proceeded to the point of obscuring and corrupting the real purposes of an institution of higher learning." The statement called for a new athletic policy which would adhere to the tenets of the Southern Association of Colleges and Secondary Schools: "Faculty control of all phases of intercollegiate athletics is required."

In the midst of the athletic turmoil on campus, Pomfret resigned as president to become director of the prestigious Huntington Library and Art Gallery at San Marino, California, from which he retired in 1966. He published a number of scholarly historical works, and at the time of his death was considered the foremost authority on colonial New Jersey history.

Dr. James W. Miller, professor and chairman of the philosophy department, was named acting president by the board of visitors in September 1951, but within a month, United States Navy Vice Admiral Alvin Duke Chandler, son of former college president Dr. J.A.C. Chandler, was named the new president. An alumnus of the college, Chandler was also a graduate of the United States Naval Academy. The board asked President Truman to relieve Chandler of his navy duties so he could assume the post immediately.

The board of visitors at once assigned Chandler the task of putting the college "ship" back on course and moving it forward. President Dwight D. Eisenhower attended Chandler's inauguration and received an honorary doctor of laws degree on May 15, 1953.

Chandler elevated the department of jurisprudence to the "Marshall-Wythe School of Law" and several legal festivities during the next few years

This photograph, believed to have been taken in 1943, shows (in rear of door) John Stewart Bryan, former college president, in his robes as chancellor of William and Mary. In front of Bryan is the new college president, Dr. John E. Pomfret. J. Gordon Bohannon, rector of the college, preceeds Pomfret. Courtesy of the Office of University Communications, College of William and Mary

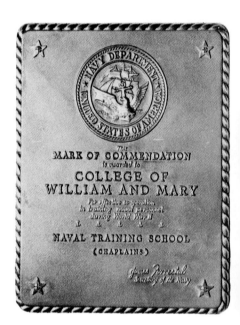

The S.S. William and Mary Victory was launched on April 20, 1945 at the Bethlehem-Fairfield Shipyard near Baltimore, Maryland. Constructed in forty-five days, the 6,000-ton ship was 495 feet long, with three decks and three masts. It had a 10,700 dead-weight tonnage and a turbine engine capable of 15.5 knots. The vessel was outfitted as a troop carrier. The captain's quarters were decorated in green, gold, and silver. At the launching, the college was officially represented by Dean of Women,

Dr. Grace Warren Landrum; Eleanor Harvey (Rennie); and Edith Harwood (Smith). Harvey, as president of the Women Students' Cooperative Government Association, was the ship's sponsor, and Harwood, the incoming WSCGA president, was the maid of honor. Other ships associated with the college were the victory ships S.S. James Blair and S.S. Lyon G. Tyler, and the U.S.S. Botetourt. Courtesy of the Office of University Communications, College of William and Mary

This plaque, located on the entry wall of James Blair Hall (formerly Marshall-Wythe Hall), commends the college for its cooperation in the training of naval personnel during World War II. Courtesy of the Office of University Communications, College of William and Mary

160

Dr. John E. Pomfret, college president (center, with diploma in hand), presides at mid-semester graduation exercises in the chapel of the Sir Christopher Wren Building on January 29, 1944. Dean of the faculty, Dr. James W. Miller (at Pomfret's left) calls the degree candidates forward. Courtesy of the Office of University Communications, College of William and Mary

From March 1943 until November 1945 the United States Navy had its naval chaplains training school stationed at William and Mary. This photograph shows the chaplains marching on the walk in front of the old library and old Rogers Hall. When the naval officers marched, students had to move aside. Courtesy of the College Archives, College of William and Mary

In February 1947 former governor of Virginia, Colgate W. Darden (above, at microphone) was formally invested as the honorary chancellor of William and Mary. Darden had been named to the post in 1946; however, he resigned a few months later to become president of the University of Virginia. To the rear of Darden are Dr. John E. Pomfret, president (laughing), and Dr. Sharvy G. Umbeck, dean of the college (behind Pomfret). Courtesy of the Office of University Communications, College of William and Mary

As a major step to provide college training for veterans, William and Mary formally took over the St. Helena Naval Berthing Facility at Norfolk on July 31, 1946. Dr. John E. Pomfret, president, signs for the property, while William M. Tuck, governor of Virginia, watches over his shoulder. The naval officers are unidentified. Courtesy of the Office of University Communications, College of William and Mary

Old Morris House is shown as it looked in the fall of 1947. The photograph was staged for a Colonial Echo cameraman. Several persons have tried to identify the men in the picture, but none has succeeded. A later rector of the college, R. Harvey Chappell, Jr., is at right holding a large knife. Morris House was a favorite residence for athletes as well as many other students. According to residents, the cost to rent a room was less than elsewhere on campus. After the house was demolished in the mid-1960s, the college bookstore was built on the site. Courtesy of the Society of the Alumni. from the 1948 Colonial Echo

On January 1, 1948, the William and Mary Indians made their first bowl appearance against the University of Arkansas in the first annual Dixie Bowl in Birmingham, Alabama. Coach Rube McCray and the Indians had a 9-1 season, losing only to the University of North Carolina. The team's co-captains were Bob Steckroth and Ralph Sazio. Before 25,000 fans, the teams exchanged leads several times before the final whistle sounded and Arkansas was a 21-19 winner. The next year the Indians, with co-captains Harry "Red" Caughron and Lou Hoitsma, went to their second bowl, the Delta Bowl, defeating Oklahoma A&M, 20-0. When this picture was taken, crowds were gathered in Birmingham to welcome the 1947 William and Mary team when it arrived several days before the game. From the 1948 Colonial Echo

William and Mary's 1947 tennis team won just about everything there was to win in the collegiate world of tennis, compiling their second straight undefeated season, running their victory streak to forty-one matches, and winning the first NCAA national championship for any college athletic team. The tennis coach was Dr. Sharvy G. Umbeck, professor of sociology and dean of the college. Members of the cham-

pionship team were, from left to right: Top row—Dick Randall, Jim Macken, Fred Kovaleski, George Fricke, and Bob Galloway. Bottom row—Bob Doll, Howe Atwater, Lyman Chennault, and Bernard "Tut" Bartzen. Not pictured is Gardner Larned, who won the national singles championship, defeating Vic Seixas of the University of North Carolina. From the 1948 Colonial Echo

The 1948 William and Mary tennis team brought the college its second straight NCAA title, and Bernard "Tut" Bartzen and Fred Kovaleski won the national doubles championship. From left to right, team members were: Back row—Howe Atwater, Bob Doll, and Bartzen. Front row—Bill Smith, Dick Randall, and Kovaleski. Courtesy of the Men's Athletic Association, College of William and Mary

The Apollo Room in old Phi Beta Kappa Memorial Hall was designed to conform to the original Apollo Room in the Raleigh Tavern where Phi Beta Kappa was formed on December 5, 1776. The portrait over the mantel is of William Short, second Phi Beta Kappa president. A fire in December 1953 destroyed the auditorium wing of the old building, but the front portion with the Apollo and Dodge rooms was saved. In 1962 the old Apollo Room became the college's president's office. Courtesy of the Office of University Communications, College of William and Mary

United States President Harry S Truman received an honorary doctor of laws degree at William and Mary on April 2, 1948 during Canadian-American Day ceremonies. Truman is being hooded by Dr. Ben McCary (left, center) and Dr. William G. Guy. Standing by are the president of William and Mary, John D. Pomfret (far left) and Rector A. Herbert Foreman. Courtesy of the College Archives, College of William and Mary

Kappa Alpha Theta sorority laughs it up at one of their parties in 1949-50. The exact event is lost in the annals of sorority lore, but the photograph appeared in the 1950 Colonial Echo

In the late 1940s, Dr. W. Melville Jones, professor of English, taught many of his classes in the Sir Christopher Wren Building, the oldest academic building still in use. Here he is lecturing on one of his favorite subjects, Milton's Paradise Lost. *Jones held numerous administrative titles before he retired in 1971; he served as dean of the faculty, dean of the college, vice president of William and Mary, and vice president for academic affairs. Courtesy of the College Archives, College of William and Mary*

Since the 1940s, college students have waited tables at a number of Colonial Williamsburg Foundation restaurants. Here students tend table in old Travis House, used as a restaurant from 1930 to 1951. Courtesy of the Office of University Communications, College of William and Mary

The William and Mary Choir led the audience in the alma mater in Blow Gymnasium on June 10, 1951, to close graduation exercises and the school's 258th year. Dr. Carl A. "Pappy" Fehr became choir director in 1945 and held the post until his retirement in 1974 as chancellor professor of music. Through the years, he built the choir to more than seventy voices. The choir's annual• tour through Virginia and the eastern United States was an important phase in its program, along with the traditional Christmas and spring campus concerts. In the late 1960s and early 1970s, Dr. Fehr initiated a Christmas television program that was seen on about forty stations from coast to coast. Courtesy of the Office of University Communications, College of William and Mary

Kappa Alpha Theta sorority had the homecoming float theme "William and Merry Go Round Richmond" for the October 25, 1952 homecoming parade. Courtesy of the College Archives, College of William and Mary

Here the Indian Mermaids of 1952-1953, forerunner to the Mermettes, synchronized swimming group of today, practice in the cozy confines of Blow Gymnasium. The program that year was a Mardi Gras water carnival. Courtesy of the College Archives, College of William and Mary

One of the largest paid attendances in the history of the stadium at Cary Field occurred in the fall of 1949 when the Indians played the University of North Carolina. The great UNC tailback Charlie "Choo Choo" Justice attracted a crowd of nearly 17,000 persons to the game, which was won by Carolina, 20-14. Courtesy of the Richmond Times-Dispatch

In the fall of 1950, excavations were made by Colonial Williamsburg Foundation architects, under the supervision of college President Dr. John E. Pomfret, a noted historian. These excavations, between Ewell Hall and the Wren Building, uncovered the remains of the foundations for the extension of the Sir Christopher Wren Building, as proposed by Thomas Jefferson in 1772. Portions of the foundations were completely intact. Courtesy of the Colonial Williamsburg Foundation

This photograph is believed to have been taken of the old Colony Room in the late 1940s or early 1950s. This smaller dining room in Trinkle Hall became "The Pub" in the 1970s and early 1980s. During the 1983-1984 renovation of Trinkle it was returned to dining room use. Courtesy of the College Archives, College of William and Mary

167

continued to attract attention to the nation's oldest college law school, founded in 1779. On September 25, 1954, Earl Warren, chief justice of the United States, and Rayner Goddard, lord chief justice of England, participated in a commemorative program beginning the bicentennial year of John Marshall's birth. Later, between February 8 and September 24, 1955, about twenty internationally known persons from the legal and judicial fields attended programs honoring Marshall.

Like his father, Chandler felt a keen interest in strengthening the business administration program and began working for an eventual school of education. Student enrollment at the college increased to 2,303 in 1959-1960, even though admission standards began to be toughened.

The time was not ripe at William and Mary for a building program like the one developed by J. A. C. Chandler, but his son realized the college facilities were being overtaxed. In 1953, Bryan Hall, a dormitory in the Bryan complex, opened for students, soon to be followed by four other units on the site of what was once Cary Field, a small athletic facility primarily used for football and baseball games. It had been replaced in 1934 when the football stadium was constructed.

Later, the new Phi Beta Kappa Memorial Hall was dedicated in 1957, replacing the older structure partially destroyed by fire in 1953. The building opened just in time to host the National Governors' Conference, held in Williamsburg as part of the 350th anniversary of the Jamestown settlement of 1607. Landrum Hall opened in 1959, named in memory of Dr. Grace Warren Landrum (dean of women and professor of English at the college, 1927-1947). It was the last building erected within the walls of the main campus. The Campus Center, housing student publications offices and related student activities, opened in 1960, but the big building boom was yet to come.

In 1957, William and Mary participated in a number of programs commemorating the 350th anniversary of the settlement of Jamestown in 1607. On October 16, Queen Elizabeth and her

This aerial view of the campus and the city of Williamsburg in February 1953 shows the old Eastern State Hospital (in lower left), College Corner (center), the campus with its women's athletic field (upper left) and the football stadium (top, center). Courtesy of the Richmond Times-Dispatch; *A. B. Rice photo*

husband Prince Philip visited Williamsburg. From the balcony of the Sir Christopher Wren Building she spoke to a large crowd in the front yard. For the former royal college, it was the first royal visit by a reigning British monarch. Chandler and his wife Louise served as hosts to the royal couple at the college; earlier they had entertained Queen Elizabeth, the Queen Mother, during her William and Mary visit in 1954.

Chandler encouraged the college to develop exchange programs with colleges and universities in England, and in 1959 The Drapers' Company in London began to provide support for an exchange scholarship.

On March 3, 1960, the Virginia General Assembly enacted a bill changing the college's name to "The Colleges of William and Mary," an act that, for a few years, changed the entire complexion of the school.

In the spring of 1953 the members of the board of visitors met in the Blue Room of the Sir Christopher Wren Building. The members included, from left to right: Mrs. Philip W. Hiden; Dr. Dowell J. Howard; Harold W. Ramsey; James Robertson (rector); William Robertson; Dr. Hudnell Ware, Jr.; and Roy Charles. Courtesy of the Office of University Communications, College of William and Mary; from the 1953 Colonial Echo

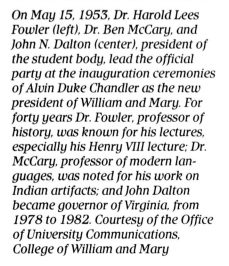

On May 15, 1953, Dr. Harold Lees Fowler (left), Dr. Ben McCary, and John N. Dalton (center), president of the student body, lead the official party at the inauguration ceremonies of Alvin Duke Chandler as the new president of William and Mary. For forty years Dr. Fowler, professor of history, was known for his lectures, especially his Henry VIII lecture; Dr. McCary, professor of modern languages, was noted for his work on Indian artifacts; and John Dalton became governor of Virginia, from 1978 to 1982. Courtesy of the Office of University Communications, College of William and Mary

United States President Dwight D. Eisenhower attended the inauguration of Alvin Duke Chandler as president of William and Mary on May 15, 1953, and brought greetings from the nation's capital. The platform was in front of the Sir Christopher Wren Building and photographers crowded in the aisle as the crowd listened to the president. *Courtesy of the* Richmond Times-Dispatch

Dwight D. Eisenhower applauds the inauguration of Alvin Duke Chandler as president of William and Mary. Eisenhower continued a long-standing tradition of American presidents coming to campus and he received an honorary doctor of laws degree. *Courtesy of the Office of University Communications, College of William and Mary*

As part of freshmen orientation week, "ducs" were required to curtsy and bow to Lord Botetourt as they passed his statue. Gail Elizabeth Bowen (left) and Eleanor Baird pay appropriate homage to the statue in September 1953. *Courtesy of the College Archives, College of William and Mary*

This aerial photograph was taken of the campus in the spring of 1954. Notice the Bryan Complex (top left area, adjacent the stadium at Cary Field), has been completed, except for the wings added in 1959. In the center portion of the campus, old Phi Beta Kappa Memorial Hall (below the Sunken Garden, to the left of the Wren Building) lost its auditorium wing in the December 1953 fire. Courtesy of the College Archives, College of William and Mary

Probably the most fascinating of all William and Mary football teams was the "Iron Indians" of 1953. Coached by Jackie Freeman, the team had only twenty-three, twenty-four, or twenty-five players, depending upon the source consulted. Nevertheless, it was one of the smallest squads ever to represent a major college. Despite the lack of manpower, the team compiled a 5-4-1 record, tying Navy and defeating Wake Forest College, Virginia Polytechnic Institute, George Washington University, North Carolina State College, and the University of Richmond. From left to right, team members were: Front row—George Parozzo, John Bednarik, Tommy Martin, Steve Milkovich, Bill Bowman, Jack Place, and Quinby Hines. Second Row—Al Grieco, Tom Hamilton, Charles Copeland, Aubrey Fitzgerald, Linwood Cox, Bob Elzey, and Jerry Sazio. Third row—Chet Waksmunski, George Karschner, Shorty Herrman, Bill Marfizo, Bill Riley, and John Risjord. Fourth row—Bill Nagy, Charlie Sumner, Sam Scott, Doug Henley, and Bill Martin. From the 1954 Colonial Echo

The auditorium of old Phi Beta Kappa Memorial Hall burned on December 29, 1953. The city firemen, under the direction of Chief Eliott Jayne, arrived as flames were breaking through the building's roof. They were able to control the blaze and prevent the fire from reaching the other half of the building, which housed the national headquarters for the Phi Beta Kappa Society and its irreplaceable records. Ironically, city firemen had staged an on-the-scene drill at the building just a few days before the fire. That drill was based on the premise of a fire starting backstage in the auditorium, which is exactly what really happened. Courtesy of Fred L. Frechette

On September 25, 1954, United States Chief Justice Earl Warren (center) and Lord Chief Justice of England Rayner Goddard participated in a program at William and Mary to commemorate the beginning of the 200th anniversary of the birth of John Marshall. The festivities also commemorated the 175th anniversary of the establishment of the first chair of law in the United States, at William and Mary in 1779. In the rear of the picture are busts of George Wythe (left), English jurist William Blackstone (center), and John Marshall (right). The third person from the left is Tom Clark, associate justice of the Supreme Court, who served as visiting lecturer in law in the late 1970s, after retiring from the court. Courtesy of the Office of University Communications, College of William and Mary

This is the business district along Duke of Gloucester Street on March 31, 1954. The old structures had been torn down and replaced with shops and stores in Neo-Georgian architecture, which harmonizes with colonial Virginia architecture throughout the town. The college can be seen at the right rear of the picture. Courtesy of the Richmond Times-Dispatch

Henry Billups, the bell ringer of the college, rides in his last homecoming parade in the fall of 1954. Billups was in his sixty-seventh year of service to William and Mary, having begun his work in 1888 when the college reopened. Courtesy of the Colonial Williamsburg Foundation

John Westberg, editor-in-chief, and Alison Sandlass, a member of the art staff, work busily on page 81 of the 1954 Colonial Echo. Other feature pages in the section are scattered on the tables of the office in Marshall-Wythe Hall (later named James Blair Hall). Courtesy of the College Archives, College of William and Mary

Queen Elizabeth The Queen Mother visited Williamsburg and came to campus on November 12, 1954. Here, the Queen Mother smiles as she accepts a gift from Ronald I. Drake, president of the student body. College President Alvin D. Chandler is standing between the Queen Mother and Drake. The presentation took place in the rear portico of the Sir Christopher Wren Building. Courtesy of the Newport News Daily Press and Times-Herald

The William and Mary Theatre opened its 1954 season on October 20 and 21 with Somerset Maugham's The Circle, which was performed in an arena setting in the small gym of Blow Gymnasium. The December 1953 fire at old Phi Beta Kappa Memorial Hall put the theatre on the road. Until the new theatre opened in 1957, large productions were staged at Matthew Whaley School in town, while other plays were at the gymnasium or in a corner of the foyer in the remaining wing of old Phi Beta Kappa Memorial Hall. The Circle had been originally scheduled for March 1953, but the fire postponed it eight months. Courtesy of the College Archives, College of William and Mary

In early June, 1956, President Alvin Duke Chandler took time to sign all the diplomas for the 1956 graduating class. Assisting him while he signed the diploma for Gray Bromleigh, Jr., of Williamsburg, was long-time administrator J. Wilfred Lambert. Miss Wilma Clark, a member of Lambert's staff, checked diplomas. Lambert, a 1927 William and Mary graduate, joined the faculty in 1931 as an instructor in psychology and became a dean in 1935. Courtesy of the Office of University Communications, College of William and Mary; Thomas L. Willliams photo

Beginning in 1930 and continuing through 1959, the annual Sunset Ceremony immediately following the commencement program was held at the gravesite of Col. Benjamin Stoddert Ewell, former college president. The memorial service honored those William and Mary alumni who had died in the past year. This photograph shows one of those services; the cemetery wall is at right. In 1961 the ceremony moved to the Sunken Garden, and in 1976 to the courtyard of the Sir Christopher Wren Building. Courtesy of the Office of University Communications, College of William and Mary

One of the highlights of the 1956-1957 William and Mary Theatre season was the production of Shakespeare's Romeo and Juliet, starring Linda Lavin and Don Smith as the ill-fated lovers. Miss Lavin (center) graduated in 1959 and went on to Broadway to star in a number of productions. She is currently the star of Alice, the CBS television comedy. During a visit to campus in the spring of 1983, she gave the William and Mary Theatre credit for the experience to launch her professional career. Courtesy of the William and Mary Theatre Archives

The brothers of Kappa Sigma fraternity were photographed at the lodge during rush week in the fall of 1956. William Wingate (right) offers a friendly hand of welcome to a potential pledge. Courtesy of the College Archives; from the 1957 Colonial Echo

Registration for classes at William and Mary has never been an easy task, even with the advent of the computer and preregistration in the 1980s. This is a view of fall registration in 1956. It was simply standing in line and trying to get classes that would fit a schedule. Courtesy of the College Archives, College of William and Mary

In the late 1950s a new college library was proposed at the end of the Sunken Gardens opposite the Sir Christopher Wren Building. This is an architectural rendering of the building that was never built. Courtesy of the Office of University Communications, College of William and Mary; Thomas L. Williams photo

PROPOSED LIBRARY
College of William and Mary
Williamsburg Virginia

In May 1957, four faculty members, and major officials in the William and Mary Theatre, stand in front of the Phi Beta Kappa Memorial Hall, the theatre's new home. From left to right they are: Roger Sherman, theatre designer; Althea Hunt, theatre founder and long-time director; Howard Scammon, theatre director; and Al Haak, theatre technical director. Courtesy of the Office of University Communications, College of William and Mary; Thomas L. Williams photo

Queen Elizabeth II of Great Britain and her husband Prince Phillip visited Williamsburg and Jamestown in connection with the 350th anniversary of the English settlement of 1607. On October 16, 1957, the queen visited campus and spoke to the students, faculty, and townspeople from the front balcony of the Sir Christopher Wren Building. On the balcony, from left to right, were: James M. Robertson, college rector; Queen Elizabeth II; Prince Phillip; and Alvin D. Chandler, college president. Courtesy of the College Archives, College of William and Mary

Approximately 20,000 persons gathered in the college yard and at College Corner to greet Queen Elizabeth in what is believed to have been the largest crowd then in the history of the city. In this picture, the queen is just getting into her carriage after speaking at William and Mary. Courtesy of the Colonial Williamsburg Foundation; George Beamish photo

The 1959-1960 basketball season recorded 15 wins and 11 defeats, with a 9-1 record in the cozy confines of Blow Gymnasium. In this photograph Bev Vaughn goes in for a layup against Virginia Tech, while guard Kenny Roberts (22) watches. Unfortunately, William and Mary lost, 92-91, but it was the only home loss of that season. In the 1960-1961 season the team was undefeated at home, 7-0. The second floor seats nearly covered the edge of the downstairs playing floor and frequently fraternity men would pound their feet against the backboard supports of the opposing team's goal. And the gym was packed for virtually every game; noise in the "crackerbox" could be deafening at times. Finally, some teams simply refused to play in the gym. Courtesy of the Office of University Communications, College of William and Mary

The big event at the beginning of second semester was sorority rush, which culminated with coeds "rushing" to their respective new houses after receiving bids to join. The event always attracted much attention on campus. This photograph shows Sorority Court on Acceptance Day, circa 1960. Courtesy of the Office of University Communications, College of William and Mary

Alvin Duke Chandler and his wife frequently entertained students and student organizations at the President's House in the 1950s. Louise Chandler had tea for Elizabeth, the Queen Mother in 1954 and Queen Elizabeth II in 1957, and was a gracious hostess on many other important college occasions. Courtesy of the Office of University Communications, College of William and Mary; Thomas L. Williams photo

178

In the winter of 1960 a jubilant Bill Chambers, head basketball coach at William and Mary, was carried off the court on the shoulders of his players after the team had defeated the University of West Virginia, 94-86. The game ended the Mountaineers' fifty-six-game winning streak against Southern Conference opposition. When he played for the college, Chambers pulled down fifty-one rebounds in a game against the University of Virginia in 1953. The mark still stands as an NCAA major college record. Courtesy of the Men's Athletic Association, College of William and Mary

For decades, through the early 1970s, graduation exercises were held on the front yard of the Sir Christopher Wren Building. These are seniors in a mid-1950s graduation. The statue of Lord Botetourt had not yet been moved. Courtesy of the Office of University Communications, College of William and Mary

For years William and Mary had three important convocations each year: opening convocation in September, spring convocation in late April, and graduation in June. In this picture, Alvin Duke Chandler (at podium) presides during this opening convocation in the late 1950s in Blow Gymnasium. Courtesy of the Office of University Communications, College of William and Mary; Thomas L. Williams photo

Chapter Twelve
1960-1985

"A New Campus of Good Arts and Sciences"

With little fanfare the Virginia General Assembly's actions in the closing minutes of the 1960 session called for an immediate reorganization of the College of William and Mary and its affiliated schools in Norfolk and Richmond. This "Greater College" would be headed by a chancellor, who would be named by an enlarged board of visitors, whose membership was increased from eleven to fifteen members.

The bill also created two new junior colleges to be established in Newport News and Petersburg, an outgrowth of existing successful extension programs: eventually they became Christopher Newport College and Richard Bland College, respectively. (In the mid-1970s, Christopher Newport College became an independent, four-year college, while Richard Bland operates today as a two-year college of William and Mary.) The chief executives of the five branches would have direct administrative responsibility for their respective campuses, but would report to the chancellor and

This photograph shows the mall in the heart of the new campus, with its many brick walks. The Robert Andrews Hall of Fine Arts is at the right. The building in the central rear is the John Millington Life Sciences Hall, and to the distant right is the new Rogers Hall. Courtesy of the Office of University Communications, College of William and Mary

through him to the board.

Within a few weeks, the visitors named Chandler the new chancellor of The Colleges of William and Mary. For the new president they looked to Richmond and selected Dr. Davis Y. Paschall, then state superintendent of public instruction and since 1957 an ex-officio voting member of the board. Paschall received his B.A. and M.A. degrees from William and Mary and his Ed.D. degree from the University of Virginia. He was inaugurated October 13, 1961, but by that time the "colleges" structure was already coming apart, being attacked by persons and groups from across the state, especially by William and Mary alumni, who did not like their college treated on a par with the newer colleges in Norfolk and Richmond.

Local Williamsburg Delegate Russell M. Carneal introduced legislation, which had been recommended by the State Council of Higher Education in Virginia, calling for the abolition of the "colleges" structure and the independence of the Norfolk and Richmond branches. Virginia Governor Albertis S. Harrison, in his first speech before the general assembly in January 1962, said, "The College of William and Mary, founded in 1693, is to all our hearts and minds a distinctive institution....A College with so rich a promise of fulfilling such a timely mission... does not have to compromise its identity and character, or bargain its name for support by this Commonwealth." An editorial headline in *The Richmond News Leader* proclaimed simply: "A Time to Walk Alone."

On July 1, 1962, the "colleges" ended. Chandler, who had been chancellor of the whole system, was elected by the visitors to the

This was the first meeting of the enlarged board of the Colleges of William and Mary. The group met on May 22, 1960 in the Blue Room of the Sir Christopher Wren Building. In this picture, President Alvin Duke Chandler is standing at the extreme left. With him, from left to right, are: Front row—H. Lester Hooker; T. Edward Temple; Davis Y. Paschall; Frank Ernst; C. K. Hutchens; and J. B. Woodward, Jr. Standing—Chandler; M. Carl Andrews; Dr. H. Hudnall Ware; James M. Robertson (rector); Dr. J. Asa Shield; John P. Harper; W. Fred Duckworth; and R. William Arthur. Not present were W. Brooks George and Edward P. Simpkins, Jr. The board's first task was to select a new president after Chandler was named chancellor of the system; Paschall was selected within a few weeks. Courtesy of the Richmond Times-Dispatch

By the early 1960s the college library had completely outgrown its facility. The primary study area was in the first room, although there were some tables among the open stacks in the rear. The library closed at 11:00 p.m. because of the curfew. Courtesy of the College Archives, College of William and Mary

One of the legendary homecoming floats was in the 1960 parade when Chi Omega sorority created their "Wedding Cake." The float was very tall and led to a rule prohibiting tall floats because of overhanging trees and the potential fire danger. Nevertheless, the wedding cake was a float to be remembered! Courtesy of the Office of University Communications, College of William and Mary

At his inauguration as William and Mary president in October 1961, Dr. Davis Y. Paschall formally installed the Queen's Guard as the ceremonial unit of the Reserve Officer Training Corps at the college. Its coat-of-arms features the phoenix, demonstrating the college's ability to rise again after disaster. Courtesy of the Office of University Communications, College of William and Mary

The Dean of the Marshall-Wythe School of Law, Dr. Dudley Warner Woodbridge, was named the recipient of the first Thomas Jefferson Award at Charter Day 1963. Woodbridge (right) had been named by Life Magazine ten years earlier as one of the five outstanding professors in America. Dr. Davis Y. Paschall (center) and Dr. Julian P. Boyd of Princeton University applaud Woodbridge's selection. Courtesy of the Office of University Communications, College of William and Mary; Thomas L. Williams photo

The Flat Hat, the student newspaper at William and Mary, received the Pacemaker Award, announced in the May 19, 1962 edition. The award named the paper one of the nation's top five student papers as judged by the Associated College Press and the American Newspaper Publishers Association. The honor appropriately came during the paper's fiftieth anniversary year. The editor was Jerry Van Voorhis, who later returned to the college, serving as assistant dean of admissions and later as assistant to the president. Courtesy of the Office of University Communications, College of William and Mary; Steve Toth photo

Near Landrum Hall, where the old campus drive circled behind Crim Dell, workmen made an intersection for a new street—the roadway which would eventually circle the academic side of the new campus. At this intersection is the entranceway to the new campus. In this picture, construction crews are cutting the road through the campus woods. Courtesy of the Office of University Communications, College of William and Mary; Thomas L. Williams photo

In the fall of 1963 the pony Wampo-Feather was ridden in the homecoming parade by Wade L. Johnson. The cheerleaders followed in the convertible pulling Wampo's trailer. Courtesy of the Office of University Communications, College of William and Mary

Virginia Governor Albertis S. Harrison addressed William and Mary commencement on June 9, 1963 in the front yard of the Sir Christopher Wren Building. Seniors in caps and gowns occupy the first rows of seats, and parents, family, and friends are in the rear. During these graduations, until the 1970s, students came forward individually to receive their diplomas. Courtesy of the Office of University Communications, College of William and Mary; Thomas L. Williams photo

In the fall of 1963 the new campus was just being developed. In this picture, the old campus with its Georgian architecture is at the lower right with Chandler and Landrum halls. Phi Beta Kappa Memorial Hall is off Jamestown Road with the women's athletic field in the foreground and the tennis courts to the rear. Campus Drive has just begun to circle through the woods and William Small Physical Laboratory (above Phi Beta Kappa) and Adair Women's Gymnasium have just been completed. Across the bridge, DuPont Hall is under construction and Yates Hall, completed in 1962, is at the upper right. Courtesy of the Office of University Communications, College of William and Mary; Thomas L. Williams photo

On January 23, 1964, Dr. Davis Y. Paschall, college president, addressed a meeting of the joint session of the state senate and the house of delegates budget committee. On that particular occasion, he never alluded to facts and figures in his budget presentation, but spoke eloquently about the college and for the first time called it "The Alma Mater of a Nation." He said the college, like the commonwealth and nation, "had been tempered by fires and wars and [had] risen from each crucible of adversity even stronger—until now it was, indeed, their Pearl of Great Price to be polished with support and devotion, and never allowed to tarnish by neglect." The committee gave him a standing ovation and went on to recommend many millions of dollars in construction funds to continue the building of the new campus. Courtesy of the Richmond Times-Dispatch

In September 1963, William S. "Pappy" Gooch, "Mr. William and Mary," formally retired. He was one of the most loved sports figures in Virginia. A University of Virginia graduate and four-sport letterman, he spent thirty-six years on the "reservation," where he coached all the men's sports at one time or another and also served as athletic director. He was business manager from 1939 to 1973. Courtesy of the College Archives, College of William and Mary

honorary post of chancellor of the College of William and Mary, joining Bryan and former Governor Colgate Darden (1946-1947) as the only chancellors named in the twentieth century. Chandler served until 1974.

When he returned to his alma mater, Paschall found more than 2,200 students on campus, attending classes in basements, attics, and World War II Quonset huts scattered about campus. No classroom buildings had been constructed since 1934, but enrollment had more than doubled. Dormitories also were crowded with students sleeping in attic rooms designed for storage. Other rooms designed for two students were being occupied by four students. Chandler earlier had recognized the same problems and had worked on expansion plans. However, during the winter of 1960-1961, it was Paschall who developed a complete plan for an expanded campus. Chancellor Chandler took the plan to the general assembly almost immediately, seeking money to implement it. The result, between 1962-1972, was the development of "A New Campus of Good Arts and Sciences," as Paschall called it.

A new library would be the apex of an academic court, with classroom buildings fanning out from the library, providing what the architects called an openness when the new campus is viewed from the front, Jamestown Road. In that decade, forty construction projects were undertaken at a cost of $36 million, plus an additional $4 million in equipment, roads, and landscaping, more than twice the amount spent on facilities by the college in its long history.

Included in the construction were ten new academic buildings and four new dormitory complexes, which included one group of buildings initially designed for sororities (now student interest housing); and one complex for fraternities. Among the buildings constructed were: Yates Hall (1962); Cornelia Storrs Adair Gymnasium for Women (1963); Jessie Ball duPont Hall (1964); William Small Physical Laboratory (1964); Earl Gregg Swem Library (1966); the William and Mary Bookstore (1966); Robert Andrews Hall of Fine Arts (1967); Commons dining hall (1967); the fraternity complex (1967); John Millington Hall of Life Sciences (1968); Hugh Jones Hall (1969); and William and Mary Hall (1971). Richard L. Morton Hall, a health center, and new sorority houses were begun.

On the main campus Paschall also oversaw renovation of a number of older buildings originally developed by President J.A.C. Chandler; Paschall's plans for the 1970-1980 decade called for the development of many of the projects constructed under the new presidential administration.

An orator of the first rank, Paschall seemed able to blend the best of two previous William and Mary presidents—Tyler's sense of history and J.A.C. Chandler's energetic building instincts—to obtain finances in larger amounts from the general asembly. For many students, however, Paschall will be remembered as providing those funds, from his discretionary accounts, to keep them in school when hard times hit; his service to people, most of which is uncharted, is another personal legacy.

When the Swem Library was completed, the statue of Lord Botetourt, which had been removed from the front campus in 1958 to protect it, was placed in a special gallery within the library. Her Brittanic Majesty's Guard, part of the Reserve Officers Training Corps initiated during the 1957 visit of Queen Elizabeth II, was formally invested by Paschall as a drill unit honoring three royal benefactors: Queen Mary II, Queen Anne, and Queen Elizabeth II.

In January 1968, the State Council of Higher Education in Virginia officially determined that William and Mary had attained a "modern university status," but should forever preserve its historic college name.

On February 8, 1968, William and Mary celebrated its 275th anniversary of the granting of the royal charter with a nationwide telephone hookup of alumni chapters throughout the country. On February 11, the Charter Day Convocation was held with addresses by the Right Reverend Honorable Robert Wright Stopford, lord bishop of London, and Sir Patrick Henry Dean, British ambassador to the United States, stressing the English founding of the college.

In 1970, a new undergraduate curriculum was implemented after a thorough two-year study by the faculty of arts and sciences. The revision, the first in thirty-five years since Bryan's revitalization of the liberal arts, emphasized a more flexible approach to the liberal arts study. By the end of 1970, the undergraduate enrollment was about 3,600 full-time students with an additional 1,000 full-time graduate students. Four new academic departments had been started in the last decade, with doctoral programs instituted in physics, marine science, education, and history and eight new master's degree programs initiated. Also

Before the new Earl Gregg Swem Library opened in 1966, a large number of library books were stored outside the confines of the old Carnegie Library on the main campus. In fact, many books were stored, like these, in the basement of the Sir Christopher Wren Building. Frequently, students had to call for a book several days in advance in order for the staff to locate it in the storage areas. Courtesy of the College Archives, College of William and Mary

In September 1965, the statue of
Lord Botetourt, which had been in
storage since the late 1950s, was
moved across campus and carefully
installed in the basement gallery of
the Earl Gregg Swem Library, which
was formally opened on Charter Day
1966. Courtesy of the Office of University Communications, College of
William and Mary; Thomas L. Williams photo

At the Charter Day program on
February 13, 1965, William and Mary
honored two long-time college
associates with honorary degrees: Dr.
Richard Lee Morton (second from
right), professor of history, and James
Robertson (third from left), who
served as rector for a decade from
1952 to 1962. Other honorary degree
recipients were Lord Harlech, British
ambassador to the United States
(second from left), and Lewis F.
Powell, Jr. (third from right), who later
became an associate justice of the
United States Supreme Court. Dr.
Davis Y. Paschall (far left), president,
and J. B. Woodward (far right), rector,
pose with the group. Courtesy of the
Office of University Communications,
College of William and Mary;
Thomas L. Williams photo

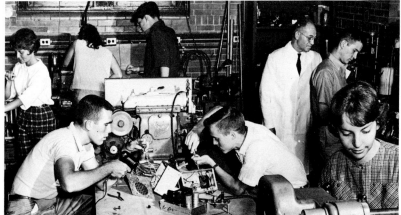

Many students who suffered through
the physics labs in old Rogers Hall in
the 1950s and 1960s, under the
worst kinds of conditions, will recall
the primitive working situations and
the cramped quarters. In this photograph, students James Teal, Sheila
Ann Thibault, Suzanne Duval, Lyndon
Wilson, Nelson Hower, Joseph Fectau,
and Betty Bright try to complete one
of the lab assignments with the help
of Mr. Hunt, the lab assistant. Courtesy of the Office of University Communications, College of William and
Mary; Thomas L. Williams photo

In November 1965 an oriental-style
bridge, painted russet and white, was
erected over the lily pond. Azaleas
and other colorful shrubs were planted and the area was named Crim
Dell, in memory of J.H. Crim (1901)
whose family provided funds for the
area's clean-up. In the foreground a
roadside railing matches the bridge.
Courtesy of the Office of University
Communications, College of William
and Mary; Thomas L. Williams photo

Probably one of William and Mary's greatest football victories came in a stunning 27-16 upset over the United States Naval Academy in 1967. Head coach Marv Levy (who later became a professional football head coach) holds the game ball triumphantly over his head at the rally of several thousand students and townspeople held when the team returned from Annapolis, Maryland. The sign in the background reads, "William and Mary, Number 1 in the East." President Davis Y. Paschall (second from rear, left) smiles his encouragement. From the 1968 Colonial Echo
In November 1967, The Virginia Gazette, Williamsburg's weekly newspaper, ran this editorial cartoon by Dick Stinely the week following the William and Mary defeat of Navy. The cartoon says it all! Copyright The Virginia Gazette

As part of the college's Christmas gift to the nation in 1967, the William and Mary Choir, under the direction of Dr. Carl A. "Pappy" Fehr, taped a thirty-minute television program of holiday music, which was presented on many stations across the country. The Christmas program became a tradition and attracted much good publicity for the college. Here Dr. Davis Y. Paschall, president, and his wife, Agnes Winn Paschall, join the choir for the taping of one segment. Courtesy of the Richmond Times-Dispatch; Thomas L. Williams photo

The Right Reverend and Right Honorable Robert Wright Stopford, the bishop of London, spoke to the 275th anniversary convocation. Dr. Davis Y. Paschall, president, is seated at his right (under the banner) with Sir Patrick Henry Dean, British ambassador to the United States, and Anthony Packe, master of the ancient Drapers' Company of London. The man at the far right is unidentified. Courtesy of the Office of University Communications, College of William and Mary; Thomas L. Williams photo

188

A large brick entryway today leads into the "New Campus of Good Arts and Sciences," as Dr. Davis Y. Paschall, college president, termed the expanded William and Mary in the 1960s. This plaque, placed at the entrance in 1968, is below a bronze cast of the phoenix, a long-time symbol of William and Mary. Courtesy of the Office of University Communications, College of William and Mary

In 1968 the Society of the Alumni established a special medallion to be presented to college guests, friends of the college, and major participants in the commemoration of the 275th anniversary of the charter of William and Mary. The medallion, created by Carl Roseberg, professor of fine arts, was given to eighty-two persons. Courtesy of the Society of the Alumni

The Drapers' Company of London, one of the city's oldest livery companies, presented this silver candelabrum to the college on February 8, 1968, the 275th anniversary of the chartering of William and Mary. The Drapers' Company was associated with the college for many years providing funds for an exchange scholars' program. Courtesy of the Richmond Times-Dispatch

From left to right, the board of visitors in 1968-1969 included: Front row—Davis Y. Paschall, president, and Walter G. Mason, rector. Second row—Ernest Goodrich, vice rector; R. Harvey Chappell, Jr.; and R. William Arthur. Third row—E. Ralph James; J. Edward Zollinger; Frank W. Cox, secretary; and Governor Thomas B. Stanley. Fourth row—John C. Swanson; Mrs. Robert V. H. Duncan; Mrs. Vernon Geddy; and Blake T. Newton, Jr. Fifth row—William R. Savage, Jr.; Russell B. Gill; Harry D. Wilkins; W. H. Bowditch; and Walter S. Robertson. Courtesy of the Office of University Communications, College of William and Mary; from the 1969 Colonial Echo

The Virginia Commission on Constitutional Revision presented its report to Governor Mills E. Godwin, Jr., on January 11, 1969 in the great hall of the Sir Christopher Wren Building at William and Mary. The commission met in the Blue Room of the Wren just prior to the presentation of the report. Godwin (at the podium) thanked the group for its effort. Joining the governor for the presentation were John Warren Cooke, Speaker of the House of Delegates (seated left of Godwin); Albertis S. Harrison, former governor, state supreme court justice, and commission chairman; and Lieutenant

Governor Fred G. Pollard (seated at right). The commission is seated immediately in front of the dais. From left to right are Dr. Davis Y. Paschall, William and Mary president; Ted Dalton, federal district judge for the Western District of Virginia; Alexander M. Harman, Jr., judge of the Virginia twenty-first judicial circuit; Colgate W. Darden, Jr., former governor of Virginia and former president of the University of Virginia; Lewis F. Powell, Jr., attorney, past president of the American Bar Association, and later associate justice of the United States Supreme Court; Albert J. Bryan, Jr., judge of the Virginia

sixteenth judicial circuit; Oliver W. Hill, attorney and former member of the Richmond city council; Hardy Cross Dillard, James Monroe, professor of law, University of Virginia (hidden by hat); J. Sloan Kuykendall, attorney, past president of the Virginia State Bar Association; George M. Cochran, attorney, former member of Virginia state senate; and A. E. Dick Howard, associate dean and professor of law, University of Virginia, commission executive-director. Courtesy of the Office of University Communications, College of William and Mary; Thomas L. Williams photo

190

In February 1966, student volunteers helped library staff members transfer all the volumes in the college library to the new Earl Gregg Swem Library on the new campus. Furniture and equipment boxes are piled in front of the new library after the installation. The library became the focal point of the new campus. Courtesy of the Office of University Communications, College of William and Mary; Thomas L. Williams photo

Republican presidential candidate Richard M. Nixon made a campaign visit to William and Mary on October 2, 1968 and spoke to a selected group of persons in the great hall of the Sir Christopher Wren Building. A group of protesters greeted Nixon when he reached the campus. Courtesy of the Richmond Times-Dispatch; Amir M. Pishdad photo

Congressman Gerald R. Ford (R-Michigan), minority leader of the United States House of Representatives, was the commencement speaker on June 9, 1968, but unlike most speakers did not receive an honorary degree. From left to right are Dr. Alfred Armstrong (faculty marshal); Ford; Dr. Davis Y. Paschall, president; Judge Sterling Hutcheson (former rector); Walter Mason (rector); and Dr. Frank Evans (faculty marshal), near right. As president of the United States, Ford was scheduled to return to the college in February 1977 for Charter Day to receive an honorary degree, but he lost his reelection bid and decided not to make the visit. Courtesy of the Office of University Communications, College of William and Mary; Thomas L. Williams photo

At the 1969 homecoming, William and Mary established its Sports Hall of Fame with the induction of thirty-four men. Athletic Director H. Lester Hooker, Jr., alumnus, conceived the idea. Twenty-eight of the honorees posed for this photograph. Kneeling, from left to right, are James Driver; Leif Scheie; H. M. Stryker; Bob Wallace, Jr. (representing his father); Otto Lowe; J. C. Chandler; Crawford Syer; and Art Matsu. Leaning over at the extreme left is Otis Douglas. In the middle row, from left to right, are Meb Davis; Billy Palese; Thomas Halligan; Joe Fleckenger; Henry M. Little; Melville "Stumpy" Bryant; Arthur B. "Bud" Metheny; and Walt Zable. In the background from left to right, are Saunders Allmond; Tommy Thompson; R. N. "Rube" McCray; George Hughes; Harlie Masters; Chet Giermak; George Rafey (representing Marvin Bass); Buster Ramsey; Glenn Knox; Al Vandeweghe; and Riley H. Cloud (representing his son, "Flying" Jack Cloud). Courtesy of the Society of the Alumni

In May 1970, during the Vietnam War, a student strike was called at William and Mary to protest the U.S. Army invasion of Cambodia and the deaths on the Kent State University campus during a student protest. In this picture the strike sign and the colonial-clad gentleman provide an interesting contrast. Courtesy of the Richmond News Leader; Thomas L. Williams photo

In October 1969, William and Mary students joined fellow collegians across the country in calling for a moratorium on the bombing of North Vietnam. Students stand here in a twenty-minute silent vigil over a coffin in front of The Brafferton. Courtesy of the Richmond Times-Dispatch

In the fall of 1969 construction had just begun on William and Mary Hall, the college's 10,000-seat athletic and convocation center. In this picture, the massive concrete exterior supports are just being poured. Courtesy of the Office of University Communications, College of William and Mary; from the 1970 Colonial Echo

In June 1970, graduation was still held in the front of the Sir Christopher Wren Building, and seniors passed through the doors of the building to the front. In this picture the procession is viewed through one of the arches on the rear portico. Courtesy of the Richmond Times-Dispatch; Don Pennell photo

Nancy Terrill (right) was elected president of the Student Association for 1969-1970, becoming the first woman elected to head the student body. She was succeeded for the 1970-1981 school year by Winn Legerton (left). The transfer of the mace occurred at commencement in June 1970. Courtesy of the Office of University Communications, College of William and Mary

The homecoming parade of 1970 featured such floats as this one created by Chi Omega sorority. It was the last parade directed by Dean of Students J. Wilfred Lambert, who had just become vice president for student affairs. The 1971 parade was rained out and the 1972 parade was directed for the Society of the Alumni by the author, who has continued as parade marshal to the present. Courtesy of the Office of University Communications, College of William and Mary

In December 1970, William and Mary's basketball team christened its new basketball facility, William and Mary Hall, against the University of North Carolina and came out on the short end of a 101-72 score. The building was not yet completed and there was no heat. North Carolina moved their Trailways bus into the back of the arena and retired to it during halftime to stay warm. Folding chairs were brought into the hall since the permanent seats had not been installed. Courtesy of the Office of University Communications, College of William and Mary

created were four schools—education, business administration, marine science and continuing studies—and in 1971 the board of visitors approved the beginning of a bachelor of business administration degree (BBA).

Paschall retired from the presidency on August 31, 1971, and Dr. Thomas Ashley Graves, Jr., associate dean of the faculty of the School of Business Administration at Harvard University, was selected the new president. After the college's first formal nationwide search by a committee of alumni, students, and faculty, the visitors made the final selection, electing Graves by one vote over alumnus Blake T. Newton, Jr., also one of the visitors.

Graves continued the building program begun by Paschall, and at one time in the mid-1970s, there was more construction on campus, worth more money, than at any other time in William and Mary's history. The sororities decided not to move into the new residences completed for them in 1972 and the buildings became the Botetourt Residences for student interest group housing. The new David J. King Student Health Center (1972) and Richard Lee Morton Hall (1973) also were projects begun during the Paschall presidency. New Graves-developed buildings included William Barton Rogers Hall (1975); the Randolph Residences (1980); the new Marshall-Wythe School of Law (1980) and the Joseph and Margaret Muscarelle Museum of Art (1983).

In addition to the new buildings, all the old dormitories on the main campus were completely renovated; old Rogers Hall was renovated and renamed Chancellors Hall to house the School of Business Administration; the old college library, renamed Marshall-Wythe in 1968 when the law school was located there, became St. George Tucker Hall in 1980, housing the English department. Numerous other building changes were undertaken to improve the organization of the administration and academic departments on campus.

In 1972, the visitors, upon the recommendation of Graves, ended a long-standing college trademark, abolishing the Extension Division, established in 1919, and eliminating the School of Continuing Studies, created in 1968. All full-time classroom and course work was to be concentrated in degree programs on the Williamsburg campus, as urged by the faculty of arts and sciences. Graves' long-stated personal goal for William and Mary was "the quest for excellence" in all areas of the

college, especially in academics and student life. Popular with the student body, Graves improved general housing and created student interest housing, including various language houses.

At the urging of Governor A. Linwood Holton, the college worked hard to secure the relocation, on William and Mary property although not adjoining the original campus, of the National Center for State Courts. With the construction of the center's building, William and Mary realized the potential for a legal center and sought funds for a new law school. The American Bar Association had threatened the college with a loss of accreditation for the law school if facilities were not improved, especially the library. Law School Dean William B. Spong, Jr., former United States senator from Virginia, worked tirelessly on behalf of the law school in securing needed financial support from the legislature, and by 1984 the school was listed by one national newspaper as one of the top thirty-six law schools in the nation.

Graves also introduced a second revival on campus in the fine arts: encouraging the William and Mary Choir to take several trips to Europe; helping establish, in 1978, the Virginia Shakespeare Festival program presenting three Shakespeare plays each summer; and supporting a larger number of major art exhibitions throughout campus.

The culmination of this activity came in October 1983, with the dedication of the first phase of the Muscarelle Museum of Art. In the spring of 1984, sufficient private funds had been raised for second-phase construction. When completed, the museum will not only have space to house major rotating art exhibitions, but also galleries for the college's own extensive art collection, including major works of eighteenth-century portraiture.

In 1977, under the aegis of Graves and his wife Zoe, a major program was initiated among friends of the college to furnish the President's House with authentic English and American antiques of the Queen Anne and Chippendale styles. Clement E. Conger, curator of the White House and curator of the reception rooms of the United States Department of State, served as chairman of the endeavor, which formally lasted for seven years. In all, the project secured more than $1 million in new furnishings for the museum-home.

Probably Graves's most significant accomplishment was the initiation in 1973 of William and Mary's only significant fund-raising program

In late September 1971, just a few weeks after Dr. Thomas Ashley Graves, Jr., assumed the duties of president of William and Mary, he was joined for this photograph in front of the President's House by Vice Admiral Alvin Duke Chandler (left) and Dr. Davis Y. Paschall, immediate past presidents of the college. Courtesy of Dr. Davis Y. Paschall; Thomas L. Williams photo

since the J. A. C. Chandler Administration and the work of Goodwin. The building of a full-time staff dedicated to raising funds from the private sector led in 1976 to the launching of a three-year campaign to raise $19 million for endowment programs in faculty professional development, student financial aid, and various enrichment programs. The drive ended in 1979 with more than $20 million raised. The annual fund-raising efforts of the college increased each year under Graves's leadership.

Statistics speak for themselves: William and Mary's endowment grew from $9.4 million in 1971 to about $32.4 million in 1983. Annual fund-raising increased from $124,612 in 1971 to more than $613,000 in 1983; total gifts to the school increased from about $271,000 in 1971 to $5 million in 1983. More than $36 million was raised in private gifts during Graves's tenure.

In December 1983, Graves announced that his tenure as president would end in the summer of 1985. However, on November 1, 1984, he said he had accepted the position as director of the Henry Francis duPont Winterthur Museum and would be leaving William and Mary in January 1985.

With several major long-range planning studies currently underway on campus. Graves had felt it was important that a new president be in place to implement those programs and to guide the college toward its 300th anniversary year in 1993.

Under the leadership of new rector Anne Dobie Peebles of Sussex County (the first woman elected rector in the history of the college), the board of visitors began a search for Graves's successor in the spring of 1984. A seventeen-member search committee, comprised of board members, alumni, faculty, and student representatives, screened nearly 200 candidates and narrowed the consideration to three persons who were offered to the board of visitors as unranked finalists: Dr. Samuel A. Banks, president of Dickinson College, Carlisle, Pa.; Josiah Bunting III, president of Hampden-Sydney College, Hampden-Sydney, Va.; and Dr. Paul R. Verkuil, dean of the law school at Tulane University.

On December 20, 1984, the board of visitors elected Verkuil on the first ballot. A native of Staten Island, N.Y., he graduated from the college with a bachelor's degree in English literature in 1961. Verkuil's wife, the former Frances Hiden Gibson, is an alumna, class of 1966. They have two children, Tara and Gibson. Prior to going to Tulane as dean in 1978, Verkuil was a member of the law faculty at the University of North Carolina at Chapel Hill, 1971-78, and practiced law for four years in New York City. He received a law degree from the University of Virginia and an advanced law degree and his doctorate in judicial science at New York University.

On Charter Day 1972 Dr. Thomas A. Graves, Jr. (center) took the oath of office as William and Mary's new president in ceremonies at William and Mary Hall. Virginia Chief Justice Harold F. Snead (left) administered the oath. Also in attendance were Governor A. Linwood Holton (second from left, now a member of the college's board of visitors); Roger L. Barnett, master warden of the Drapers' Company of London (second from right); and Ernest Goodrich, rector of the college (far right). Courtesy of the Office of University Communications, College of William and Mary; Thomas L. Williams photo

The old Bright house, once the Kappa Alpha fraternity house, and later the old college apartment house, became the new Alumni House in 1972. W. Brooks George, a former rector of the college, headed the fund-raising drive. Officially cutting the ribbon to open the facility were (from left to right): C. Randolph Davis, president of the Society of the Alumni; Dr. Thomas A. Graves, Jr., president; W. Brooks George; Dr. Davis Y. Paschall, president emeritus; and Gordon C. Vliet, executive vice president of the society. Courtesy of the Society of the Alumni; Thomas L. Williams photo

The Alumni Medallion, the highest award the Society of the Alumni can bestow on its own, was given in October 1971 to six recipients. From left to right they were: Dr. J. T. Baldwin, Dr. Janet Coleman Kimbrough, and Walter J. Zable; Dr. Thomas A. Graves, Jr., college president, and Pamela Pauley Chinnis, first woman alumni society president); and Gregory G. Lagakos, Earl B. Broadwater, and W. Walker Cowles. Courtesy of the Society of the Alumni; Thomas L. Williams photo

The Order of the White Jacket was established at William and Mary in 1972 to recognize those persons who had served as waiters in the college dining room during their student years. A number of the returning members of the order at homecoming 1976 posed on the steps of Blow Gymnasium. Courtesy of the Office of University Communications, College of William and Mary; Thomas L. Williams photo

In 1960, Richard Bland College in Petersburg was created as a two-year school under the auspices of William and Mary. James M. Carson (right front), was its first president. On June 1, 1973, Carson presided at his last commencement and Bland's twelfth. Former William and Mary president and chancellor Alvin Duke Chandler (front left) gave the commencement address. Bland continues today as a two-year school under the William and Mary board of visitors, and Dr. Clarence Maze is president. Courtesy of the Richmond Times-Dispatch; *Bob Jones, Jr., photo*

Just before the end of classes in May 1972, the Colonial Echo *yearbook was produced. Edited by Harriett Stanley, the book was produced by an effort of 111 students, with a core of 30 senior staff members. As Ms. Stanley explained, the objective of the yearbook was to recover from the bad image of 1971 and to rank among the nation's top annuals, but to rank on imagination, rather than conformity to present journalistic notions. The book did just that, winning the 1972 Columbia University award as the top yearbook in the*

country. In succeeding years, the Colonial Echo; *the* Flat Hat, *the student weekly newspaper; and the* William and Mary Review, *a literary magazine, have won numerous national awards in the Columbia University contest, the Associated Collegiate Press contest, and the Society for Collegiate Journalists contest, where the* Echo *also was the national winner in 1975 and 1976. Here 1971-1972 staff members gather to be photographed. Ms. Stanley is in the the center, pointing with her hand. From the 1972* Colonial Echo

In January 1972, William and Mary received a major bequest from Jay Winston Johns of Charlottesville, including many hundreds of acres of property and the "cabin castle" home of United States President James Monroe, an alumnus of the college. Significant renovations were made at the home and it was reopened to the public under the auspices of the college. The William and Mary board of visitors made a tour of the facility in 1978. Courtesy of the Office of University Communications, College of William and Mary

In the spring of 1976, the Society for Collegiate Journalists at the college, formerly Pi Delta Epsilon, honorary journalism fraternity, established an annual journalist in residence program. Roger Mudd, then White House reporter for CBS-TV news was the initial visiting journalist and the society awarded him the William and Mary Heritage Award for Excellence in Journalism. Courtesy of the Office of University Communications; Lyle Rosbotham, photo

In the spring of 1972 William and Mary Theatre actress Glenn Close (left) performed in Phi Beta Kappa Memorial Hall as Alice in You Can't Take it With You. Jeff West portrayed Tony. Close performed in a number of other productions and went to Broadway immediately after graduating Phi Beta Kappa in June 1974. In 1984 she won significant acting distinction by being nominated for an Oscar Award for the movie The Big Chill; a Tony Award for the Broadway play The Real Thing; and an Emmy Award for the television movie, Something About Amelia. She won the Tony as best actress of the year. A number of actors and actresses who have come from William and Mary Theatre in the past twenty-five years have been successful in television and motion pictures. From the 1972 Colonial Echo

President Gerald Ford and his wife Betty (right) and Jimmy Carter and his wife Rosalynn meet on the stage of Phi Beta Kappa Memorial Hall following the third presidential debate on October 21, 1976, just two weeks before the election. Courtesy of the Newport News Daily Press *and* Times-Herald

Evangelist Billy Graham used William and Mary Hall as the scene for his July 4, 1976 bicentennial program to America. In this picture, Graham (at podium) is preaching his sermon as television cameras focus on him and the audience. Courtesy of the Office of University Communications, College of William and Mary

William and Mary students, faculty and townspeople gathered at William and Mary Hall to view the third presidential debate October 21, 1976. The hall was packed with 10,000 persons and both candidates visited the crowd immediately following the debate. President Gerald Ford gives Virginia Governor Mills E. Godwin, Jr., the "OK" sign as his daughter Susan (left) and singer Pearl Bailey (right) look on. Courtesy of the Office of University Communications, College of William and Mary

The third presidential debate of 1976 took place at Phi Beta Kappa Memorial Hall on the William and Mary campus. Students in the Bryan Complex prepared a large sign to welcome President Gerald Ford and Governor Jimmy Carter. Courtesy of the Richmond Times-Dispatch; *Don Rypka photo*

On December 5, 1976 the Phi Beta Kappa society held its triennial meeting at William and Mary in honor of the founding of the organization at the college on December 5, 1776. Attending the program was former college president, Dr. John E. Pomfret (left), and his wife Sarah (second from right), who met with William and Mary President Dr. Thomas A. Graves, Jr., and his wife Zoe. Courtesy of the Office of University Communications, College of William and Mary

Jimmy Carter speaks before the special podium at William and Mary Hall during the 1976 debate. It was his only visit to the campus. Courtesy of the Office of University Communications, College of William and Mary; Lyle Rosbotham photo

Carter O. Lowance, former executive vice president of William and Mary and executive assistant to six Virginia governors, received an honorary degree on February 13, 1977 at the college. Attending the program and offering congratulations to Lowance (third from right), the man they called "little governor," were five former Virginia governors. From left to right were Colgate W. Darden; A. Linwood Holton; J. Lindsey Almond; Lowance; Mills E. Godwin, Jr.; and Albertis S. Harrison. Courtesy of the Newport News Daily Press and Times-Herald

Two cows graze on the front yard of the Sir Christopher Wren Building at William and Mary in much the same manner depicted in the famous 1840 watercolor of the campus by Thomas Millington. The cows, and a later milking demonstration, were part of a 1976 April Fool's Day reenactment of the Millington tableau. Taking part in the milking demonstration were Dr. Thomas A. Graves, Jr., president, and Virginia Secretary of Commerce and Natural Resources Earl Shiflett. Courtesy of the Richmond News-Leader; Thomas L. Williams photo

The women's athletic fields have been preserved in order to retain a large green area. The field was named in memory of Martha Barksdale, one of the first women to graduate from William and Mary and for more than forty years a member of the faculty and the department of women's physical education. Courtesy of the Office of University Communications, College of William and Mary; Thomas L. Williams photo

William and Mary coeds annually seek opportunities to sunbathe. For many years, Barrett Beach (the top rear porch at Barrett Hall) was a favorite spot to get a great tan. In recent years, young women have sought the sun's rays behind the brick walls that surround much of the main campus. These coeds are sunbathing between Jefferson Hall and Barrett in front of the colonnade. Courtesy of the Richmond Times-Dispatch; photograph by the author

In the spring of 1977, William and Mary physics professors Dr. Hans C. von Baeyer (left) and Dr. John L. McKnight developed a "Lecture on Natural Philosophy." Delivered in the style of an eighteenth century lecture and employing a reproduction of a period frictional electrostatic generator, the professors focused on the science of physics at the time of the American Revolution. The presentation was given throughout the eastern United States for a number of years and is now given occasionally to special groups. Courtesy of the Colonial Williamsburg Foundation

The 1977-1978 William and Mary cheerleaders were into jumping, vaulting, and other stunts that were beginning to become part of the cheerleaders' repertoire. Members of the group were: Patty Gilboy (captain), Linda Anderson, Jane Clemmer, Wanda Davis, Sheryl Meyer, Patty Pfeiffer, Cathy Welch, Sam Eure, Jerry Evans, Lester Limerick, Jim Schwarz, Glen Smith, Greg Stallings, and Andy Wampler. Courtesy of the Men's Athletic Association

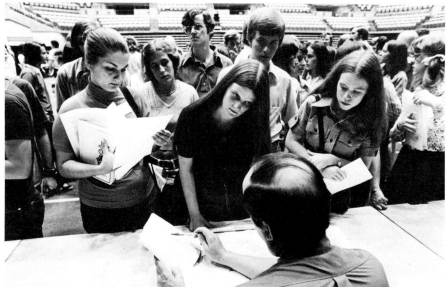

For years registration meant students standing in line for hours in an effort to get the courses they wanted. Now there is a computerized pre-registration, but there are still lines for freshmen and transfer students. This photograph, taken circa 1978, shows students signing up with Dr. Frank T. Lendrim for courses in the department of music. Courtesy of the Office of University Communications, College of William and Mary

At the 1978 homecoming the William and Mary marching band posed for this group photograph in the Sunken Garden. Long-time band director Charles R. Varner (far right) continued to lead the group. It played at all home football games and portions of the band began playing for the basketball games. The concert band continued to give its major spring concerts and go on spring tour to New York City. Varner, professor of music, retired in June 1984 after a well-respected career. Courtesy of the Office of University Communications, College of William and Mary

In February 1979, the William and Mary board of visitors considered a proposal to expand the stadium at Cary Field to as many as 30,000 seats in order to maintain Division IA football standing. Students and faculty voiced major concern over the proposal. On February 10, about 1,800 protesters tried to get the board's attention, some carrying signs. No stadium expansion took place and eventually William and Mary was designated a Division I-AA school by the NCAA. Courtesy of the Richmond Times-Dispatch; Bill Lane photo

In September 1980, the Marshall-Wythe School of Law moved into its newly completed multimillion-dollar facility adjacent to the National Center for State Courts. As dean of the law school, William B. Spong, Jr. (former United States senator from Virginia) helped greatly to obtain the funding for the facility from the Virginia General Assembly and in moving the school into a major position among law schools in America. In the spring of 1984, USA Today listed the school among the top thirty-six law schools in the country.

In the lobby of the new Marshall-Wythe School of Law are two restored stained glass windows given in 1980 to William and Mary by All Souls College, Oxford University. This window is of Sir Christopher Wren, believed to have designed the first college building of 1695. The other window is of William Blackstone, the great English legal scholar. The old windows were removed at All Souls College during the bombing in World War II; they were not replaced. Dr. William F. Swindler, John Marshall professor of law, helped secure them for William and Mary. Courtesy of the Richmond Times-Dispatch; photograph by the author

The Society of the Alumni expanded its merchandising operation in the late 1970s and early 1980s and offers a large variety of items with the William and Mary cypher or coat of arms. Courtesy of the Society of the Alumni; Thomas L. Williams photo

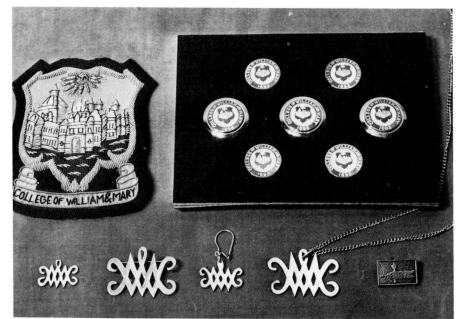

In 1981 the William and Mary women's golf team won the AIAW Division II National Championship, the first national title in women's sports. From left to right, the team members were: Back row—Debbie Spencer, Ann T. Lambert (coach), and Tracy Leinback. Middle row—Mary Wilkinson and Wendy Rilling. In front, Mary Ellen Fedor holds the team championship trophy. Courtesy of the Women's Athletic Association, College of William and Mary

This aerial photograph was taken in the winter of 1980 and shows the colonial campus (bottom); the main campus, with the Sunken Garden and the Georgian academic buildings and dormitories; and the new campus with its more modern architectural design (top and above left). College Corner is at the "V" at the bottom and William and Mary Hall is at the top right. Courtesy of the Office of University Communications, College of William and Mary

In the 1980s, members of Kappa Sigma fraternity's "white" brigade liven up the basketball games at William and Mary Hall with their cheering and yelling. The organization, which sits together just off the playing floor, single-handedly created the basketball cheer, T-R-I-B-E, Tribe! *Courtesy of the Men's Athletic Association, College of William and Mary*

Since 1935 students have enjoyed the Sunken Garden in various ways. In the fall of 1980 one professor decided to hold his class session outdoors in the garden. The garden is one of the more interesting added features of the William and Mary campus. *Courtesy of the* Richmond Times-Dispatch

One of the annual highlights of homecoming is the appearance at halftime of the alumni band. The band practices the Saturday morning before the game and goes through its paces, often missing other homecoming activities just to put on the show. *Courtesy of the Office of University Communications, College of William and Mary*

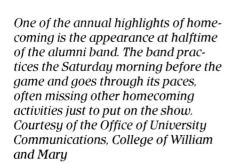

On May 4, 1981, His Royal Highness the Prince of Wales visited William and Mary to receive an honorary fellowship from the college. Founded by the English crown, the college has retained its royal charter and therefore can grant a fellowship, as well as an honorary degree. The prince became a fellow at the college for his lifetime. The convocation was held at Phi Beta Kappa Memorial Hall, where the Prince of Wales gave a brief speech and signed the 1,000,000th volume for the Earl Gregg Swem Library. At the prince's right is Dr. Thomas A. Graves, Jr., president, and to his left is Virginia Governor John N. Dalton, a college alumnus, class of 1953. *Courtesy of the* Richmond Times-Dispatch; *Gary Burns photo*

The William and Mary campus police department has grown from a one-man night security force in the 1950s to a comprehensive department with investigators and patrolmen. In this 1982 picture, a policeman on a motorcycle rides in stark contrast to the colonial Sir Christopher Wren Building in the rear. Courtesy of the Office of University Communications, College of William and Mary

The Office of Minority Student Affairs puts out extra effort to help the college admissions office recruit more black students for William and Mary. In July 1984, Dr. Thomas A. Graves, Jr., president of the college, said in his thirteenth annual report to the board of visitors that one of his regrets during his presidency was that more black students were not enrolled on campus. Courtesy of the Office of University Communications; Lyle Rosbotham photo

The newest way to get more space in a dorm room in 1982 was to build lofts within the room; sleeping space above, living space below. From left to right in this picture, taken in Barrett Hall, are: Top—Linda Wood and Toni Chaos. Bottom—Stephanie Marenick, Jenanie Springer, and Chris Tuckermori.

The Queen's Guard at the college continues to provide pomp and ceremony at appropriate college functions. Here members of the unit serve as honor guard at the Sunset Ceremony during homecoming. The program is a memorial to those alumni who have died in the past year. Courtesy of the Office of University Communications, College of William and Mary; Lyle Rosbotham photo

In 1982, homecoming brought a new type of parade entry from Kappa Sigma fraternity, which unveiled its precision lawnmower drill team. It drew rave reviews from the crowd along the parade route, which that year was changed to just one time up Duke of Gloucester, instead of the previous longer route down the street to the capitol building and back to College Corner. Courtesy of the Office of University Communications, College of William and Mary.

The Botetourt Chamber Singers were formed in the late 1970s as a select group from the William and Mary Choir, then under the direction of the popular Dr. Frank T. Lendrim. They perform at special functions and during the choir's annual Christmas and spring concerts. This photograph is of the 1982-1983 chamber group. From left to right the women are: Michelle Jacobs, Laura Ingram, Gretchen Hines, Anne Foster, Susan Hatton, Donna Dixon and Nancy Packer. The men are: William Williams, Dennis Ramsey, Patrick Wagner, Kendall Kerby, David Dowler, Lendrim (director), Richard Hoffman, James Hill, and Dirk Brown. Courtesy of the Office of University Communications, College of William and Mary

About 1:00 a.m. on January 20, 1983, a fire broke out in Jefferson Hall, built as a women's dormitory in 1921. Through the efforts of the residence hall staff and students, everyone was evacuated without injury, but the flames consumed nearly three-quarters of the inside of the structure before firemen brought it under control. This photograph was taken at sunrise, with several Jefferson residents standing in the foreground, wrapped in blankets. College insurance covered the building and the Virginia General Assembly appropriated about $70,000 to cover students who did not have insurance protection for their belongings. Courtesy of the Richmond Times-Dispatch; Associated Press photo

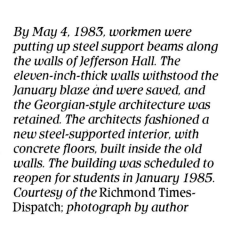

By May 4, 1983, workmen were putting up steel support beams along the walls of Jefferson Hall. The eleven-inch-thick walls withstood the January blaze and were saved, and the Georgian-style architecture was retained. The architects fashioned a new steel-supported interior, with concrete floors, built inside the old walls. The building was scheduled to reopen for students in January 1985. Courtesy of the Richmond Times-Dispatch; photograph by author

During Memorial Day weekend, 1983, Colonial Williamsburg and William and Mary served as hosts for the Summit of Industrialized Nations. William and Mary Hall was transformed into the international press center and the basketball floor became one large press room. Tables were installed, photography, and television platforms were erected, and yards and yards of drapery material and bunting were hung. On May 31, 1983, President Ronald Reagan came to William and Mary at the close of the economic summit. Accompanied by the heads of governments from the attending nations, Reagan spoke about the accomplishments of the meeting. A large walnut platform was built especially for the speech. Courtesy of the Office of University Communications, College of William and Mary

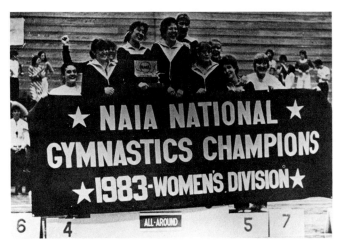

William and Mary women's sports won its second national championship in 1983, capturing the NAIA National Gymnastics title. From left to right are Jan Roltsch, assistant coach; team members Lori Pepple, Mary Ellen Williford, Nanae Fujita, Gloria Maritote, Karen Irvin, Lynn Rosenberry, Julie Stefaniw, and Lynn King; and Sylvia Shirley, head coach. Courtesy of the Women's Athletic Association, College of William and Mary

Window panes on the rear of the Sir Christopher Wren Building form individual frames for this gathering in the building's courtyard. Courtesy of the Office of University Communications, College of William and Mary

Built in 1926, Trinkle Hall had not been used by students for about a decade prior to being renovated in 1983-1984. Work on the old dining room was rushed to completion so the senior class could hold the graduation dance in the renovated building in May 1984. The building will become an annex to the Campus Center and house many offices and facilities for student activities. Courtesy of the Office of University Communications, College of William and Mary

In the mid-1970s graduation exercises were moved from the front yard of the Sir Christopher Wren Building to the air-conditioned, spacious William and Mary Hall. The 1984 commencement program was attended by nearly 10,000 persons, including more than 1,300 undergraduate and graduate students receiving degrees. Courtesy of the Office of University Communications, College of William and Mary

Beginning in the 1970s, the fiftieth anniversary graduating class was invited back to William and Mary to attend May graduation exercises and to be inducted into the Olde Guarde. In May 1984, members of the class of 1934 returned to campus and were special guests at commencement. Courtesy of the Office of University Communications, College of William and Mary

The Virginia Institute of Marine Sciences (VIMS) at Gloucester Point became part of William and Mary in 1979. In the 1930s, Dr. Donald Davis, professor of biology, established the college's department of marine science. The organization flourished, becoming one of the nation's major marine science institutes, playing a vital role in the study of the Chesapeake Bay and its tributaries. VIMS was recently under the direction of Dr. William J. Hargis, Jr., and is currently run by Dr. Frank Perkins, who is also dean of the college's school of marine science. In late June 1984, VIMS dedicated its newest building, Watermen's Hall (far right). Courtesy of the Virginia Institute of Marine Science, Bill Jenkins photo

When snow decorates the new campus, the sidewalks on the mall paint an unusual pattern. In the rear (from right) are William Small Physical Laboratory; Hugh Jones Hall; and Richard Morton Hall. Courtesy of the Office of University Communications, College of William and Mary

In October 1983, the Joseph and Margaret Muscarelle Museum of Art was dedicated. The museum, the first building on the new campus to be built entirely from private funds, is located adjacent to Phi Beta Kappa Memorial Hall and was designed by Carlton Abbott of Abbott and Associates of Williamsburg. The museum attracts much attention with its multi-colored solar wall. Called "Sun Sonata," the color design was by Gene B. Davis of Washington, D.C. The first phase cost about $1 million and approximately $1.4 million was raised for the second phase, which is scheduled to begin in 1985. Courtesy of the Joseph and Margaret Muscarelle Museum of Art, College of William and Mary; Fred Miller photo

Dr. George R. Healy became vice-president for academic affairs at William and Mary in 1971 and was later named provost. On January 9, 1985, he became the fifth acting president in the college's history, serving between the terms of presidents Graves and Verkuil. In this photograph Healy is talking to A. Linwood Holton, a member of the board of visitors and former governor of Virginia. Courtesy of the Office of University Communications, College of William and Mary; S. Dean Olson photo

Anne Dobie Peebles of Sussex County, class of 1943, was named rector of the college in February 1984, becoming the first woman elected to the post in the 291-year history of William and Mary. She served as chairman of the board's presidential search committee in 1984. Through the years she has been recognized for her public service and as a confidant of Virginia governors. Courtesy of the Richmond Times-Dispatch, Bob Brown photo

New William and Mary president Dr. Paul R. Verkuil and his wife, Frances, are shown in their New Orleans home. Known for their festive entertaining, the Verkuils were the subject of an extensive newspaper story in 1983 published in the Chicago Sun-Times. Dr. Verkuil, dean of the law school at Tulane University, was expected to assume the college presidency about July 1, 1985. Courtesy of Paul and Frances Verkuil

The rear courtyard of the Sir Christopher Wren Building is shown, with the great hall wing (left) and the college chapel (right). Courtesy of the Office of University Communications, College of William and Mary

This is the front yard of the colonial campus today. Courtesy of the Office of University Communications, College of William and Mary

The rear balcony of Barrett Hall, on the main campus, provides an interesting frame for Washington Hall in the background. Courtesy of the Office of University Communications, College of William and Mary

William and Mary Hymn
by Jeanne Rose, '33

Beneath thy trees, within thy halls,
Dear College, we give praise to thee,
To pledge ourselves, whate'er befalls—
To pledge unfailing loyalty,
Our Hearts are with thee, dear William and Mary,
However far we stray.
Our noble College, hear us now—
Thy children sing to thee today!

Dear College, old in years and fame
And richly old in honors, too.
Time shall not dull the shining name
Whose gleam our songs will e'er renew.
And as years go by, dear William and Mary,
Thy fame will never cease
But each new year rejoice to see
Thy children's praise to thee increase.

O thou, our guardian and our guide,
Renew our courage every hour,
And keep thy spirit by our side
To Aid us with its watchful power.
Throughout all our lives, dear William and Mary,
We pledge our loyalty.
Dear College, now and evermore the children cry
"All hail to thee!"

Epilogue

"It would ill behoove me to attempt here a recitation of the glories of this college and of its alumni. If there be any among you who has not a better knowledge than I of the details of this great record, I commend you to a little home study. Because, let us not forget that man takes pride in a brilliant past. There is inspiration in attempting to live up to the records established by those who have gone before us—in the family, and in institutions."

—President Dwight D. Eisenhower
May 15, 1953 at William and Mary

* * * * *

"I would hope that this institution and all in it, will always accept the challenge of trying valiantly, of daring greatly, so that the charge given us by those early leaders will be carried out fully, to the everlasting glory of this old college and all who love it.

"And at the same time, we must never lose the sense of proportion, the perspective that enables us to view events over the long reach of history, confident that come what may, this old College will endure.

"Around her proud and noble head will break storms of strife and discord, contention and dispute, but this old College will endure....

"And from these portals graduates will go forth into every nook and cranny of this great nation, bearing the indelible mark of William and Mary on their minds, their characters, their very souls...and when they long for the snows of yesteryear, they will look back with pride, pleasure and satisfaction, resting secure in the knowledge that whatever else befalls, down through the ages, this old College will endure."

—Dr. Edward E. Brickell, Rector
Homecoming Oration, October, 1979

Bibliography

Primary Sources

College papers; faculty minutes (1865-1934); and visitor's minutes (1865-1970); from the Special Collections Division, College Archives, Earl Gregg Swem Library, College of William and Mary.

Books

Bray, William, ed. *Diaries of John Evelyn*, 4 vols. London, 1872.

Burnet, George. *Bishop Burnet's History of His Own Time*. London, 1838.

Carson, Jane. *James Innes and His Brothers of the F.H.C.* Williamsburg: Colonial Williamsburg Foundation, 1961.

Chapman, Ann West. "The College of William and Mary, 1849-50: The Memoirs of Silas Totten." Master's thesis, the College of William and Mary, 1978.

Dabney, Virginius. *Virginia the Old Dominion*. New York: Random House, 1978.

_____. *Mr. Jefferson's University, A History*. Charlottesville: University Press of Virginia, 1981.

Dashiell, Thomas Grayson. *A Digest of the Proceedings of the Conventions and Councils in the Diocese of Virginia*. Richmond: Wm. Ellis Jones, 1883.

Goodwin, Mary R. M. *The College of William and Mary*. Williamsburg: The Colonial Williamsburg Foundation, 1967.

_____. *The President's House and the Presidents of the College of William and Mary, 1732-1975*, 2 vols. Williamsburg: Mary M. Goodwin, 1976.

_____. *William & Mary College Historical Notes*, 3 vols. Williamsburg: The Colonial Williamsburg Foundation, 1954.

Hamilton, Elizabeth. *William's Mary, A Biography of Mary II*. New York: Taplinger Publishing Co., 1972.

Harrison, Margaret Scott. *Commissary James Blair of Virginia: A Study in Personality and Power*. Master's thesis, College of William and Mary, 1958.

Hunt, Althea, ed. *A Chronicle - the William and Mary Theatre*. Richmond: The Dietz Press, 1968.

Jennings, John M. *The Library of The College of William and Mary in Virginia, 1693-1793*. Charlottesville: The University Press of Virginia, 1968.

The Inauguration Ceremonies at Williamsburg, Virginia May 15, 1953. Williamsburg: The College of William and Mary, 1953.

Morpurgo, John E. *Their Majesties' Royall Colledge: William and Mary in the Seventeenth and Eighteenth Centuries*. Williamsburg: The College of William and Mary, 1976.

Osborne, Ruby Orders. *The College of William and Mary in Virginia, 1800-1827*. Ed.D. thesis, College of William and Mary, 1981.

Robb, Nesca A. *William of Orange a Personal Portrait, The Later Years, 1674-1702*. New York: St. Martin's Press, 1966.

Rouse, Parke, Jr. *James Blair of Virginia*. Chapel Hill: University of North Carolina Press, 1971.

_____. *Cows on the Campus: Williamsburg in Bygone Days*. Richmond: The Dietz Press, 1973.

_____. *A House for a President, 250 Years on the Campus of the College of William & Mary*. Richmond: The Dietz Press, 1983.

Servies, James A. *Earl Gregg Swem A Bibliography*. Williamsburg, The College of William and Mary in Virginia, 1960.

Smith, Russell T. *Distinctive Traditions at the College of William and Mary and Their Influence on the Modernization of the College, 1865-1919*. Ed. D. thesis, College of William and Mary, 1980.

Trosvig, Ida. *The Study and Teaching of History in the College of William and Mary*. Master's thesis, College of William and Mary, 1938.

Tyler, Lyon G. *Williamsburg—The Old Colonial Capitol*. Richmond: Whittet & Shepperson, 1907.

Voorhees, Oscar M. *The History of Phi Beta Kappa*. New York: Crown Publishers, 1945.

Whiffen, Marcus. *The Public Buildings of Williamsburg: Colonial Capital of Virginia*. Williamsburg: Colonial Williamsburg, 1958.

Wren Society, 20 vols. London: Oxford, 1940.

Pamphlets, Articles, Speeches, and Scripts

Adams, Herbert B. "The College of William and Mary: A Contribution to the History of Higher Education, With Suggestions for Its National Promotion." Washington, D.C.: Government Printing Office, 1887.

Bryan, John Stewart. "Thomas Roderick Dew." *Bulletin of the College of William and Mary* (1939).

Bridges, Herbert Lee. "The Seven Wise Men." William and Mary *Gazette* (April 1936).

Butler, Solomon R. and Walters, Charles D. "The Life of Julian Alvin Carroll Chandler and his Influence on Education in Virginia." Hampton: Hampton Institute Press, 1933.

"Catalogue of the College of William and Mary in Virginia From its Foundation to the Present Time" (1859).

"A Commemorative Booklet, The Two Hundred and Seventy-Fifth Year." Williamsburg: College of William and Mary, 1968.

Cooley, E. J. "William and Mary in early 1900s." *William and Mary Alumni Gazette* (May 1961).

Dupuy, Monica M. "The Indian Serenaders." *William and Mary Alumni Gazette* (May 1979).

Evans, Frank B. "The Story of The Royal Charter of The College of William and Mary." Williamsburg: The Botetourt Bibliographical Society, 1978.

Ewing, Galen W. "Early Teaching of Science at the College of William and Mary in Virginia." Williamsburg: College of William and Mary, 1938.

Goodwin, Rutherfoord, "The Reverend John Bracken." *Historical Magazine of the Protestant Episcopal Church* (December 1941).

"John Evelyn, the Diarist, and his Cousin Daniel Parke II." *The Virginia Magazine* (July 1970).

Jones, W. Melville. "A President and Six Masters." *William and Mary Alumni Gazette* (May 1961).

Kale, Wilford. "Brafferton Sits Silent Beside Storied Old Wren." *William and Mary Alumni Gazette* (October 1966).

_____, ed. "Private Homes of Williamsburg...Today." Williamsburg: College of William and Mary, 1974.

_____. "Robert Andrews." *William and Mary Alumni Gazette* (July/August 1980).

_____. "The Remaking of The Wren Building." *William and Mary Alumni Gazette* (January/February 1982).

_____. "One Discreet and Fit Person." *William and Mary Alumni Gazette* (July/August 1982).

Kelly, James S. "The College of William and Mary 1960-1962." *William and Mary Alumni Gazette* (August 1962).

Lambert, J. Wilfred. "Parents Day" speech, Williamsburg, May 6, 1967.

_____. "A History of the College of William and Mary." Television script, November 23, 1968.

Malone, Dumas. "Jefferson Goes to School in Williamsburg." *The Virginia Quarterly Review* (Autumn 1957).

Millar, John Fitzhugh. "Wren: A Retrospective at 350." *William and Mary Alumni Gazette* (January/February 1984).

Molineux, Will. "House of Giants." *William and Mary Alumni Gazette* (May 1964).

_____. "On the Campus." *William and Mary Alumni Gazette* (March 1960).

_____. "The Battle of Williamsburg, 'A Most Sanguinary Engagement.'" *William and Mary Alumni Gazette* (July/August 1983).

Moore, Thomas C. and Shield, James Asa. "Medical Education in America's First University." *The Journal of Medical Education,* Vol. 44, no. 4 (April 1960).

Oberly, James W. "Saturday Night Live: Literary Societies at William and Mary." *William and Mary Alumni Gazette* (January/February 1983).

Paschall, Davis Y. "The College of William and Mary, Highlights of Progress 1960-1970, A Report on the Decade and a Look Ahead to 1970-1980." Williamsburg: The College of William and Mary, 1970.

Quittmeyer, Charles L. "The Development of Business Administration As A Field of Study at William and Mary with Related Observations." School of Business Administration, College of William and Mary, 1984.

Rouse, Parke, Jr. "The Rebirth of the Fine Arts." *William and Mary Alumni Gazette* (January/February 1981).

_____. "'Old Buck' A Hero in Spite of Himself." *William and Mary Alumni Gazette* (January/February 1983).

Shewmake, Oscar L. "The Honorable George Wythe, Teacher, Lawyer, Jurist, Statesman." Williamsburg: The College of William and Mary, 1954.

"A Statement by the Faculty of the College of William and Mary." Williamsburg: College of William and Mary, September 17, 1951.

"Statue of Lord Botetourt, Governor of the Colony of Virginia, 1768-1770." Williamsburg: Earl Gregg Swem Library, 1977.

Sweig, Donald M. *"Vert A Colledge Argent....," A Study of the Coat-of-Arms and Seals of the College of William and Mary in Virginia.* Williamsburg: 1976.

Thomson, Robert Polk. "The Reform of the College of William and Mary, 1763-1780." Philadelphia: The American Philosophical Society, 1971.

"Vital Facts, A Chronology of the College of William and Mary." Williamsburg: 1983.

Watson, Lucille McWane. "William Short, America's First Career Diplomat." *William and Mary Alumni Gazette* (July/August 1982).

Weeks, Ross L., Jr. "Gallery of Founding Fathers." *William and Mary Alumni Gazette* (July/August 1980).

"Williamsburg in the Civil War." Williamsburg: Williamsburg Civil War Committee, 1961.

Appendix

Rectors of the College of William and Mary
compiled and researched by
Wilford Kale

The Reverend James Blair, James City County	1693-1695
Miles Cary, Warwick County	1695-1696
John Smith, Gloucester County	1696-1697
The Reverend Stephen Fouace, York County	1697-1698
unknown	1698-1702
William Byrd I, Henrico County	1702-1703
Governor Francis Nicholson, Williamsburg	1703-1704
Miles Cary, Warwick County	1704-1705
Governor Francis Nicholson, Williamsburg	1705
unknown	1706-1709
Colonel William Randolph, I, Henrico County	1709
Lieutenant Governor Alexander Spotswood, Williamsburg	1711-1712
The Reverend James Blair, Williamsburg	1712
unknown	1713-1715
Lieutenant Governor Alexander Spotswood, Williamsburg	1715-1716
Philip Ludwell, James City County	1716
unknown	1717-1728
The Reverend James Blair, Williamsburg	1728-1729
Richard Kennon, Charles City County	1729
unknown	1730-1736
Henry Armistead, Williamsburg	1736
unknown	1737-1757
William Lightfoot, Charles City County	1757
*Peyton Randolph, Williamsburg	1758-1759
Lieutenant Governor Francis Fauquier, Williamsburg	1759-1760
unknown	1760-1766
*Dudley Digges, York County	1766-1767
*James M. Fontaine, Gloucester County	1767-1769
Governor Norborne Berkeley, baron de Botetourt, Williamsburg	1769-1770
unknown	1770-1771
Governor John Murray, Earl of Dunmore	1771-1772
unknown	1772-1779
*Judge John Blair, Williamsburg	1779-1781
unknown	1781-1787
Samuel Griffin, Williamsburg	1788-1789
*St. George Tucker, Williamsburg	1789-1790
unknown	1790-1812
Robert N. Nelson, Williamsburg	1812-1813
*Robert Saunders, Sr., Williamsburg	1813-1814
William Browne, Williamsburg	1814-1815
Robert G. Smith, Richmond	1815
unknown	1816-1817
James Semple, Williamsburg	1817
unknown	1818-1820
*Burwell Bassett, Williamsburg	1820-1821
unknown	1821-1825
William Browne, Williamsburg	1825
unknown	1826-1827
*John Tyler, Williamsburg	1827-1828
*John Page, Williamsburg	1828-1829
unknown	1829-1836
*Edmund Ruffin, Prince George County	1836-1837
*Thomas Martin, James City County	1837-1839
*Robert McCandlish, Williamsburg	1839-1840
*United States President John Tyler, Williamsburg-Washington, D.C.	1840-1842
*Thomas G. Peachy, Williamsburg	1842-1844
*Robert McCandlish, Williamsburg	1844-1845
*John B. Christian, Williamsburg	1845-1846
*Robert McCandlish, Williamsburg	1846-1848
*John Tyler, Charles City County	1848-1862
no incumbent during the Civil War (Tyler died in office in 1862)	1862-1865
The Right Reverend John Johns, Alexandria	1865-1869
*William H. McFarland, Richmond	1869-1871
*James Lyons, Richmond	1871-1883
*Judge W. W. Crump, Richmond	1883-1890
*General William B. Taliaferro, Gloucester County	1890-1892
*Colonel William Lamb, Norfolk	1892-1906
*Robert Morton Hughes, Norfolk	1906-1918
James Hardy Dillard, Charlottesville	1918-1940
*George Walter Mapp, Accomac	1940-1941
*J. Gordon Bohannon, Surry County	1941-1946
*A. Herbert Foreman, Norfolk	1946-1948
*Oscar L. Shewmake, Richmond	1948-1952
*James M. Robertson, Norfolk	1952-1962
*James Sterling Hutcheson, Boydton	1962-1964
J. Brockenborough Woodward, Jr., Newport News	1964-1966
*W. Brooks George, Richmond	1966-1968
Walter G. Mason, Lynchburg	1968-1970
*Ernest Goodrich, Surry County	1970-1972
*R. Harvey Chappell, Jr., Richmond	1972-1976
*John Rochelle Lee Johnson, Chadds Ford, Pa.	1976-1978
*Edward E. Brickell, Virginia Beach	1978-1982
*Herbert V. Kelly, Newport News	1982-1984
*Anne Dobie Peebles, Sussex County	1984-

*Known Alumni

(There was a reorganization of the board of visitors and from 1892-1906 there was a rector of the college and a president of the board of visitors at the same time with the board president being the principal officer of the board and the rector representing the group of visitors selected under provisions of the royal charter. Board Presidents were: General William B. Taliaferro, Gloucester County, 1892-1898; Dr. John W. Lawson, Isle of Wight, 1898-1905 and Robert Morton Hughes, Norfolk, 1905-1906.)

Presidents of the College of William and Mary

James Blair, Anglican clergyman	1693-1743
William Dawson, Anglican clergyman	1743-1752
William Stith, Anglican clergyman	1752-1755
Thomas Dawson, Anglican clergyman	1755-1760
William Yates, Anglican clergyman	1761-1764
James Horrocks, Anglican clergyman	1764-1772
John Camm, Anglican clergyman	1772-1777
James Madison, Episcopal bishop	1777-1812
John Bracken, Episcopal clergyman	1812-1814
John Augustine Smith, physician/educator	1814-1826
William H. Wilmer, Episcopal clergyman	1826-1827
Adam Empie, Episcopal clergyman	1827-1836
Thomas Roderick Dew, political economist	1836-1846
Robert Saunders, attorney/mathematician	1847-1848
John Johns, Episcopal bishop	1849-1854
Benjamin Stoddert Ewell, educator	1854-1888
Lyon Gardiner Tyler, historian/attorney	1888-1919
Julian Alvin Carroll Chandler, educator	1919-1934
John Stewart Bryan, newspaper publisher	1934-1942
John Edwin Pomfret, dean/historian	1942-1951
Alvin Duke Chandler, vice admiral	1951-1960
Davis Young Paschall, educator	1960-1971
Thomas Ashley Graves, Jr., educator	1971-1985
Paul Robert Verkuil, lawyer/educator	1985-

Robert Saunders also served as acting president, 1846-1847; Bishop John Johns initially was elected president in 1847 by the board of visitors, but declined to serve; Benjamin Stoddert Ewell served as acting (pro-tem) president, 1848-1849; R. S. Buchanan, vice rector of the board of visitors, was elected president in 1888, but declined to serve; Dr. Kremer J. Hoke served as acting president, February 8-April and April to June 1934 while Chandler was ill and shortly after Chandler's death; Dr. James W. Miller, dean of the faculty, served as acting president, August-September 1952; and Dr. George R. Healy, provost, served as acting president between the administrations of Graves and Verkuil.

Chancellors of the College of William and Mary
(Elected by the Board of Visitors)

Henry Compton, bishop of London	1693-1700
Thomas Tenison, archbishop of Canterbury	1700-1707
Henry Compton, bishop of London	1707-1713
John Robinson, bishop of London	1714-1721
William Wake, archbishop of Canterbury	1721-1729
Edmund Gibson, bishop of London	1729-1736
William Wake, archbishop of Canterbury	1736-1737
Edmund Gibson, bishop of London	1737-1748
Thomas Sherlock, bishop of London	1749-1761
Thomas Hayter, bishop of London	1762
Charles Wyndham, earl of Egremont	1762-1763
Philip Yorke, earl of Hardwicke	1764
Richard Terrick, bishop of London	1764-1776
George Washington, president of the United States	1788-1799
John Tyler, former president of the United States	1859-1862
Hugh Blair Grigsby, historian	1871-1881
John Stewart Bryan, former president of the college	1942-1944
Colgate W. Darden, Jr., former governor of Virginia	1946-1947
Alvin Duke Chandler, former president of the college	1962-1974

Presidents of the Society of the Alumni

1842-1846	Thomas Roderick Dew	1928-1929	James Hurst
1846-1847	Robert Saunders	1929-1930	Robert Murphy Newton
1847-1888	unknown	1930-1932	Frank Armistead
1888-1890	William Booth Taliaferro	1932-1934	Amos Ralph Koontz
1890-1892	Beverley Bland Munford	1934-1937	Joseph Ewart Healy
1892-1983	Robert Morton Hughes	1937-1940	Sidney Bartlett Hall
1893-1894	William W. Reynolds	1940-1942	Bathurst Daingerfield Peachy, Jr.
1894-1895	John Allen Watts	1942-1944	Walter Finnall Cross Ferguson
1895-1897	William Gustavus Jones	1944-1947	Wayne Carr Metcalf
1897-1898	Samuel Gordon Cumming	1947-1949	Vernon Meredith Geddy
1898-1900	Joseph Wells Southall	1949-1951	Carroll Brown Quaintance
1900-1902	Henry Breckinridge Wilmer	1951-1952	Charles Malcolm Sullivan
1902-1904	Julian Alvin Carroll Chandler	1952-1953	W. Sterling King
1904-1905	Percy Summerell Stephenson	1953-1955	William G. Thompson, Jr.
1905-1907	James Bankhead Tayler Thornton	1955-1956	W. Brooks George
1907-1908	John Weymouth	1956-1957	Aubrey L. Mason
1908-1910	William Churchill Lyons Taliaferro	1957-1958	John R. L. Johnson, Jr.
1910-1911	James Southall Wilson	1958-1960	Henry Irving Willett
1911-1912	Oscar Lane Shewmake	1960-1962	Robert Stanley Hornsby
1912-1913	Henry Jackson Davis	1962-1964	Robert Harvey Chappell, Jr.
1913-1914	Joseph Virginius Bidgood	1964-1965	George D. Sands, Jr.
1914-1915	James Smith Barron	1965-1966	Harry Day Wilkins
1915-1916	John Baynham Terrell	1966-1967	Alphonse Felix Chestnut
1916-1918	Henry Denison Cole	1967-1969	Dixon Littlebury Foster
1918-1919	Oscar Lane Shewmake	1969-1971	Pamela Pauly Chinnis
1919-1920	Alvan Herbert Foreman	1971-1975	Colin Randolph Davis
1920-1921	John Weymouth	1975-1977	Jean Canoles Bruce
1921-1922	James Edward Wilkins	1977-1978	Harriet Nachman Storm
1922-1923	Walter Edward Vest	1978-1979	Denys Grant
1923-1925	Channing Moore Hall	1979-1981	John H. Garrett, Jr.
1925-1926	William Churchill Lyons Taliaferro	1981-1983	Marvin F. West
1926-1928	Henry Lester Hooker	1983-1985	Austin L. Roberts III
		1985	S. Warne Robinson

Index

This photograph of the front yard of the college shows the Sir Christopher Wren Building, the statue of Lord Botetourt, and the Spotswood Cannon before 1959 when the statue was removed. Courtesy of the Office of University Communications, College of William and Mary

A lover of history and the College of William and Mary, Wilford Kale has spent more than half of his life in and around the college and its campus. He is a William and Mary alumnus and graduate of Park College in Kansas City, Missouri with a B.A. degree in history. Kale has spent countless hours roaming through the College Archives in search of information on forgotten professors and rectors, and letters and treasures from the past.

A native of Charlotte, North Carolina, Kale is currently Williamsburg bureau chief of the *Richmond Times-Dispatch,* a post he has held since 1971. He served a tour of duty in the United States Army as public information officer for the First Signal Brigade. Kale has been extremely active in many professional journalism efforts, serving as president of the Richmond Professional Chapter, Society of Professional Journalists, Sigma Delta Chi, and he is the organization's deputy regional director for Virginia. He served eight years on the board of the Society for Collegiate Journalists, and was national president of the student journalism group from 1979 to 1981.